TWO AUGUSTANS

RICARDO QUINTANA

Two Augustans

John Locke
Jonathan Swift

The University of Wisconsin Press

Published 1978

The University of Wisconsin Press
Box 1379, Madison, Wisconsin 53701

The University of Wisconsin Press, Ltd.
70 Great Russell Street, London

First printing

Printed in the United States of America

For LC CIP information see the colophon
ISBN 0-299-07420-X

Si multiples et si variées que soient les situations historiques concrètes, les visions du monde n'expriment pas moins la réaction d'un groupe d'êtres *relativement constants* à cette multiplicité de situations réelles. La possibilité d'une philosophie et d'un art qui gardent leur valeur au delà du lieu et de l'époque où ils sont nés, repose précisément sur le fait qu'ils expriment toujours la situation historique *transposée* sur le plan des grands problèmes *fondamentaux* que posent les relations de l'homme avec les autres hommes et avec l'univers.

Lucien Goldman, Le Dieu caché

CONTENTS

Introduction
Locke, Swift, and the Augustan Age
page 1

John Locke
Augustan Perspectives Old and New
page 19

Jonathan Swift
In Defence of Order
page 69

---

vii

Introduction

Locke, Swift,
and the Augustan Age

1

The present book has taken shape in accordance with two closely associated purposes which I have had in mind from the start. I have wanted, in the first place, to study Locke and Swift as two outstanding figures of the Augustan age—a period here taken, it should be noted, as one extending from the Revolution of 1689 down to about 1745[1]—and to do so from a variety of viewpoints that would allow some breadth of exploration. Both of the essays that follow are addressed to the general reader. If the objection arises, as it very well may, that there no longer exists any such creature as the general reader, one may resort to a transformational tactic and make clear those who are not being addressed. The essay on Locke is obviously not intended for professional philosophers, and the study devoted to Swift is not designed for the experienced literary scholars and critics of academia. In each of these pieces an effort has been made, however, to reflect—to reflect, let it be emphasized, not to summarize—pertinent contributions of recent scholarship.

My second desire has been to contribute insofar as I can to a clearer understanding of some of the attitudes and strains of thought present in Augustan culture. There have been innumerable studies dealing with the historical events of this age and with its literature and thought, and a number of generalizations have come to be widely accepted about the

Augustans and Augustanism. It is always in season, however, to approach this or any distinctive sector of our documented civilization less through the sanctioned generalizations that command attention and more through what the period meant as experienced reality to those then living. Neither Locke's interests and his sense of what the pressing issues of the time were nor Swift's characteristic responses to the human situation as it presented itself to him in the course of his life tell us everything about the Augustan age, but what they do tell has a validity in terms of actual experience that our generalizations, however accurate they may be in their way and helpful as they so often are, cannot lay claim to. It is always well to remember that before a cultural age ever becomes an intellectual concept entertained by us today it was what was being experienced in manifold ways by people of that period.

2

Locke and Swift fully qualify as Augustans, since it was not until 1688/89 that Locke became a published writer, most of his work appearing between that date and 1706, two years after his death, while Swift's writings were coming out in the course of the first four decades of the eighteenth century. Both of them, however, derived from the seventeenth century in an intellectual and moral sense. That they did so is significant, serving to remind us that in seeking to understand the Augustan temper and frame of mind we must take into account various factors that constituted a direct inheritance from a period antedating the Revolution of 1689. In the case of Locke it can be said that most of his central ideas are to be referred to certain historical situations that had arisen in seventeenth-century England. Swift's curious combination of conservatism regarding intellectual and religious matters on the one hand, and on the other, political convictions no less liberal than Locke's, points similarly to the formative influence of a pre-Augustan era.

The fact that Locke and Swift were in many ways rooted in

seventeenth-century soil is not wholly overlooked in the two studies that follow, but at the cost of some occasional repetition we may at this point address the subject in a more direct manner.

The areas of Locke's thought in which seventeenth-century elements are especially in evidence[2] include those that center in, first, his empiricism, second, his concept of the nature and function of what he called "reason," a concept reflecting the Anglican theory of the *via media,* and third, his political principles.

As for Locke's empiricism,[3] two somewhat different aspects of it come to light when it is considered, as it should be, against the background of seventeenth-century English thought. The late Arthur O. Lovejoy, preeminent in his day in the field of the history of ideas, wished to substitute for the study of romanticism the study of what he perceived as romanticisms. If there are not as many empiricisms as there probably are romanticisms, there is at least the sort of empiricism that is basically little more than the insistence upon the observation of facts and the application of what we thus learn to practical ends, and then there is the empiricism which is a formulated philosophy. Locke came to intellectual maturity at a time when there was great interest among many Englishmen in empiricism of the first order, which by substituting painstaking observation of the phenomena of nature for the increasingly discredited teachings of scholasticism, held forth the promise of exciting discoveries that would give man hitherto unrealized powers to control his environment, if not indeed his destiny in this world. Locke was directly influenced by this widespread movement favoring the new empirical approach; he can in fact be said to have been an empiricist in the informal sense throughout his career. His medical studies fell within an established empirical tradition, and the emphasis he placed in all his endeavors on practical, public ends showed his empirical bent.

It so happens that when Locke set to work composing his great *Essay Concerning Human Understanding* he proceeded to develop a full-fledged philosophy of empiricism, at the basis of which lay a theory of knowledge according to which all we know or can know originates from our sense impressions of the outer world; there are no innate ideas. It is Locke's theory of knowledge from which has stemmed the line of philosophic empiricism that extends through Berkeley, Bishop Joseph Butler, Hume, John Stuart Mill in the nineteenth century, and onward to certain figures of our own time.[4]

But to return to the empiricism of a practical kind. This, so far as England is concerned, had its origin in Bacon, who set forth in a way that fired the imagination of his contemporaries his great plan for the investigation of natural phenomena, to the end that the human estate might be advanced. Enthusiastic disciples of his took up the cause, and during the 1640-60 period, during the Puritan regime, many of the intellectual Puritans took part in the movement designed to promote Baconian ideals.[5] The study of natural phenomena furthered one's awareness of the divine creator of the universe; the reform of education in ways suggested by Bacon and others like Comenius could give learning a practical emphasis; the enhancement of human welfare could prepare the worldly scene for the Second Coming. The growth of science in seventeenth-century England is by no means to be attributed solely to Baconianism. But the Baconian vision persisted, and it was shared by many men who were neither Puritan nor, in the scientific sense, declared Baconians, and when the Royal Society was officially established at the Restoration, Bacon was recognized by some if not all the members as a kind of patron saint. By this time, however, an empirical mode of procedure had established itself beyond any need of Baconian authority. Robert Boyle (1627-91), the distinguished chemist and physicist, while not to be described as a Baconian, insisted upon the direct observation of physical phenomena, and Thomas Sydenham (1624-89), foremost among the early-modern students of clinical medicine, stressed reliance on firsthand observations. It is significant that Locke, as an interested scientist, was at various times associated with both Boyle and Sydenham.

But the weakness in the kind of empiricism we have just been speaking of lay in its lack of a theoretical framework. Cartesian natural philosophy, mathematical, rational, deductive, offered scientists just such a framework with its concept of regulated cosmic forces, and for this reason there were many scientists in England who were at this time primarily Cartesian in orientation.[6] The result was that two different strains were present in the English scientific scene of the period, one strain that of informal empiricism, often directed towards immediately practical ends, the other of a formal natural philosophy. The appearance in 1687 of Isaac Newton's famous work, the *Principia*—its title as Englished was "The Mathematical Principles of Natural Philosophy"— marked the beginning of a new era alike for the scientists and for the English public generally,[7] for both of whom Newtonianism supplied a comprehensive view, established rationally, that seemed to bring the whole cosmic system into focus. In an interesting and helpful article entitled "The Decline and Fall of Restoration Science" (in *Past and Present*, no. 4 [Nov. 1958], 71–89), Margaret 'Espinasse has pointed out that before the *Principia*, the sciences dependent chiefly on observation and induction had not been regarded as basically separate from the sciences of a mathematical and mainly deductive character; thereafter, the nonmathematical sciences lost out to those of the mathematical-deductive character represented by the lofty Newtonianism that commanded the attention of the eighteenth century.

How does all this bear on Locke? In his "Epistle to the Reader," which stands as a preface to the *Essay Concerning Human Understanding,* he pays tribute to such master-builders of the age as "the incomparable Mr. Newton, with some others of this strain," but states frankly that his own method is not theirs; though aiming at truth and usefulness, he has proceeded "in one of the meanest ways" as an "under-labourer in clearing the ground a little, and removing some of the rubbish that lies in the way of knowledge . . ." If Locke perceived any important differences between his own work and that of the master architects, he did not choose to dwell on them.

It may seem that what is in the nature of an expanded footnote on empiricism in England and Locke's involvement in it has extended to an ungraceful length, but it should be borne in mind that the subject is one which, considering its important ramifications, cannot be presented even in barest outline in much shorter space. Fortunately the matter of "reason" as entertained by Locke can here be dealt with much more briefly. For an understanding of Locke it is of quite as much importance as the forms of empiricism, but it is touched upon in the ensuing essay on him in a way that calls for little amplification at this point. The concept of the *via media* was one that held great appeal for seventeenth-century Anglicans, placed as they saw themselves between extreme Puritanism on the one hand and Roman Catholicism on the other. Those at both ends of the religious spectrum were reliant, so it seemed, on sheer faith—in the case of many puritan nonconformists on irrational trust in the promptings of religious enthusiasm, while on the part of Roman Catholics on trust, said to be similarly unsupported by reason, in what their church imposed. Anglicanism, it was held, was distinguished by the fact that the faith it embraced was one that rested on grounds firmly established by means of reason—by a process, that is, of examination and reasoning. Locke's empiricism, both informal and philosophical, can be said to have carried with it a recognizably similar concept of reason; reason as an instrument of analysis was as much a part of it as were the impressions of the senses. This attitude of Locke's towards "reason" and the attitudes which the Anglican principle of the *via media* implied are to be remembered when we undertake to characterize the Augustan climate of opinion. The assumption often met with that the Augustans generally were inclining towards a corrosive, skeptical rationalism overlooks this deeply implanted sense of a kind of reason that yielded acceptable knowledge and belief.

The manner in which Locke's political thought took form long before the appearance in 1689 of his *Two Treatises of Government* and his first *Letter Concerning Toleration* made him the spokesman of Revolution principles is, like his concept of reason, covered in sufficient detail in the essay devoted to him. What we may call Locke's liberalism,[8] which became the liberal tradition of the eighteenth century, was born of events dating from the time of Charles II and his successor, James.

The question of Swift's seventeenth-century inheritance likewise merits a brief discussion here, the more so since it is not taken up in any thoroughgoing way in the Swift essay. The chief points to be made concern his reaction to the new learning that had come into prominence during the seventeenth century; his whole-hearted acceptance of the Anglican *via media,* an acceptance which gave rise to what can almost be called his guiding ideology; and his political thought, whig in theory and—ultimately—tory in practice.

His relations to the intellectual currents set in motion by Baconianism, Cartesianism, and the ensuing interest in both practical and theoretical science were those of an old-fashioned conservative. If the human scene made anything plain it was man's desperate and perpetual need of more vision and self-discipline. What availed the new philosophies that professed to be extending human knowledge and promoting materialistic welfare? There was a streak of stubborn anti-intellectualism in Swift, and this has turned many people against him. If his refusal to accept new fashions in the fields of science and learning needs justification, it can be found in his unsurpassed sense of the comic futility attending some of the projects undertaken in the name of science—in the third book of *Gulliver's Travels* we are told of a project dedicated to discovering a way to turn marble into pincushions—and in his more profound and often tragic sense that men perpetually allow themselves to be diverted by the superficial appearances of things from the realities that ought to be their foremost concern. He considered both Cartesianism and Locke's empiricism, as the latter was developed in the *Essay,* to rest on a false epistemology which rejected the traditional theory of knowledge that had served from Aristotle's time down to modern days and had assumed that what existed in the world of nature was truthfully conveyed to us through the senses with the cooperation of normal reason. He seems to have exempted Bacon from much of his criticism, perceiving him, rightly enough, as one who did not question the older epistemology; he probably also admired him for his encouragement of genuinely practical science.[9]

Swift's adherence to Anglicanism was not a purely intellectual matter, but his intellectual assent to the Church's defined position is everywhere apparent. His hatred of the men who had sought to destroy the Church when the Puritans had ruled the land during the 1640s and 1650s and the suspicion with which he never ceased to regard the nonconformists of his own time may have been obsessional, but to his hatred and suspicion he brought intellectual justification. The theory of the *via media* is woven into the fabric that constitutes *A Tale of a Tub*. The corruptions in religion and learning that are being tracked down in this extraordinary satire are all manifestations of the enthusiasm and false inspiration that Anglicanism repudiated. He was familiar with the work of those seventeenth-century English writers who had analyzed religious enthusiasm at length and had delivered repeated warnings against the irrationality it encouraged.[10] If to Locke the *via media* suggested a reason that defined the grounds of knowledge and tenable belief, for Swift it enforced another sort of reason—a reason which, as in the old-fashioned faculty psychology, meant a capacity to control the irrational desires flowing from the imagination.

It is interesting, when considering Locke and Swift solely as individuals, to mark the various seventeenth-century strains of thought apparent in them. But Locke and Swift were not alone among the Augustans in reflecting certain attitudes and ideas that had been generated during the half-century or more preceding the Revolution. It is the presence of such presuppositions that places Augustanism in general—which means the outlook and temper exhibited by a preponderant number of articulate Augustans—in a somewhat different perspective from that in which both critics and common readers have long viewed it. The subject of Augustanism is one that comes quite naturally to our attention as we study

Locke and Swift. Though it scarcely calls for extended treatment in a study of the present sort, there are certain aspects
which are apropos. These are glanced at in the next section.

3

The background of dominant ideas and concepts against
which we have come to place the Augustans is that of the
Enlightenment. The matter, however, is not so simple as it
once appeared, for the reason that there are in effect two
backgrounds in question here, two Enlightenments, we may
say, and they are to be distinguished from each other no
matter how much they seem to overlap and at points to
coalesce. One is the Enlightenment as found on the Continent
during the eighteenth century; the other is to be thought of as
the English Enlightenment, which though it extended through
the eighteenth century, had its beginnings in the seventeenth
and by the time of the political revolution of 1689 was coming
into full flower. In studying the Augustans we are well
advised to bear in mind constantly the distinctive nature of
the Enlightenment as it developed in England, carrying with
it factors not present in the same degree, and some not at all,
in Continental thought.

The Enlightenment on the Continent we commonly think of
as an intellectual movement occurring chiefly in France and
deriving largely from eighteenth-century French thought.
And according to popular and long-standing opinion it was
primarily an expression of the new rationalism which had
evolved in the wake of the Renaissance and was realizing its
full potentiality in the eighteenth century—a rationalism that
sought to bring time-honored beliefs and principles to the test
of the unassisted and all-powerful faculty of human reason.
Deism now came of age, religious skepticism flourished. Philosophic materialism; the naturalization of everything pertaining to the nature of man and to the universe of which he was a
part; rationalistic criticism directed against every aspect of the
Establishment, religious, political, social—all these were pro-

moted by the radical intellectualism that marked the period.
And at the end of the road lay the French Revolution, the
practical consequence of this ferment of ideas, the final unsettling of long-sustained forms and values. In short, the Enlightenment was compounded of all the trends of thought
denounced with such vehemence by Burke in his *Reflection on
the Revolution in France* and his other manifestos appearing in
the 1790s.

Such at least are what in the past have generally been taken
to be the outstanding characteristics of the Enlightenment—
of the Enlightenment, that is, instinctively associated, though
not always explicitly so, with events on the Continent. During
our own century, however, interest in the history of ideas has
risen markedly, and the Enlightenment has been the subject
of constant analysis. The entire movement has in consequence been thrown open to what has in some cases proved to
be radical reappraisal. One has only to glance through such
casebooks on the Enlightenment as those edited by Jack
Lively (1966) and L. M. Marsak (1972) to see how specialized
the study of eighteenth-century currents of thought has become and along how many different lines of inquiry it has
proceeded. Lively, for instance, lists eight different topics of
major importance which have defined themselves as a result
of the further attention that has been given to the documents
of the period and the ideas that held the interest of educated
minds. The topics he lists are the Enlightenment's view of
itself, rationalism, empiricism, epistemology and psychology,
religion, optimism and the problem of evil, the political solutions, and progress and history.

Yet despite the increasingly sophisticated analysis of an
Enlightenment essentially Continental, it is still seen by some
of the experts and by the public generally in terms not greatly
different from those prevailing in the past. And among
people whose interest lies primarily with the English cultural
scene, there are many who still assume that the eighteenth
century in England, like the corresponding period abroad,
was predominantly an age of critical rationalism. A. D. Rit-

chie, for instance, in his *British Philosophies* (1950), a brief
and in most respects admirable survey, lends weight to such a
view. After Newton and Locke, England is said to have
suffered a radical change involving deism, the dilution of
theism, the rejection of the supernatural and the miraculous,
and a new intellectual materialism that tended to reduce
everything to mechanism that was self-running. "For the first
time in the history of English thought," Ritchie writes, "secular-
ism became intellectually respectable and fashionable." All, in
a way, doubtless true; substantiating details are not lacking.[11]
Yet such a summary view is open to question.[12] Things fall into
place in this way, it would seem, only when the full character of
the native English Enlightenment is left out of the picture and
it is assumed that what is thought of as the Continental pattern
holds for the English scene.

There is general agreement that by the end of the seventeenth century a new spirit had taken hold in England. Contemporaries recognized it even if their reactions differed. It
was a refining age—such was one uneasy comment—
"wherein all things seem ready to receive their last turn and
finishing stroke" (John Norris in the Preface to his *Miscellanies*
[1687]). On the other hand the authors of the *Spectator* papers, Addison especially, communicated a sense of an invig-
orating springtime in the social and intellectual life of the
nation. One may say that by the early years of the Augustan
age the great cultural shift under way since the Renaissance
period was, as far as the English were concerned, pretty much
of an accomplished fact. For France and the Continent generally the Enlightenment still lay ahead. It had in a very real
sense already come to England.

The English version of the Enlightenment can be traced
back to a root system that had been developing steadily
during the seventeenth century. The current of practical
empiricism has already been mentioned in connection with
Locke. The scientific movement, under the combined
influence of Baconian empiricism and the deductive systems
proposed by Descartes and others, advanced steadily. Even
the scientists who did not count themselves Baconians bore

something of the spirit of those who put the uncommitted observation of nature before any a priori theories. They shied away from dogmatism, their pursuit of the truth having something in common with the search for the grounds of rational religious belief. The kind of reason that was central to the concept of the Anglican *via media* became an important factor in the emerging cluster of assumptions and beliefs. This was not the reason of doctrinaire rationalism, not a weapon of destructive criticism, not that which gave sanction to programs for the restructuring of society; rather, it was the means whereby firm grounds of knowledge and belief could be established and the search for truth be regulated. The deists of Swift's day and later have sometimes been given an importance they do not really deserve. They wrote much and succeeded in provoking a vast amount of controversy, but their positive influence during the Augustan period was not telling; were it not for the voluminous publications put forth by their host of opponents and the alarm so often expressed in these writings historians would scarcely have seen in them a significant force. The critical rationalism of the deists was more in accord with the ideology of the French *philosophes* than with the intellectual and emotional temper predominant among the English.

The feeling, widespread at the turn of the century, that England had moved into a new age can be directly attributed to the political events that had culminated in the Bloodless Revolution of 1689, which saw the departure of James II from the native scene, the accession of William and Mary to the throne, the fashioning of a limited monarchy with specific limitations placed on the royal powers, and the Toleration Act of 1689, which at least lessened, though it did not entirely resolve, the tension between dissent and Anglican conformity. In the popular mind, freedom and liberty had been established once and for all as prerogatives of every man. Myth was mixed with reality, but the fact is that eighteenth-century Englishmen of all classes boasted of the blessings they enjoyed under a form of government unique among the Western nations. On the Continent there was general approval; in

France the *philosophes* in their schemes for the reform of their own government and society were directly inspired by the English achievement.

The fact that from the political struggles of the post-Restoration era then issued a stable society in which the different interests and classes were held in a workable balance goes far to explain the character of English Enlightenment in its mature stage. The rationalistic, ideological criticism of social and political institutions was scarcely in evidence in Augustan England and minimally so later on in the century. Though Christian belief was sometimes challenged and the Church attacked as a self-interested institution, abrasive views on such matters found no wide appeal in a society used to the concept that the truths of religion received support from reason.

It should not be supposed that all was now harmonious. The political situation brought about by the Revolution presented many problems, as rival interests and parties maneuvered for position and sought to determine the nature and extent of their power. The electorate was being continually appealed to; as J. H. Plumb reminds us in his *Growth of Political Stability in England: 1675-1724* (1967), there were more general elections between 1689 and 1715 than in the rest of the century. Nor is the air of peacefulness and complacency sometimes attributed to the Augustans confirmed by what we now know about the details of the social and intellectual life at the time. How to deal with the indigent, whose numbers were large, was still the discomforting and unsolved problem that it had been since the Tudor period. The agricultural interest, deeply entrenched in established ways and conservative, non-urban values, felt threatened by the mercantile and business interest that was rapidly attaining new importance and power. Among the men of ideas there existed widely different theories concerning human nature and the springs of human behavior. Some, in reaction against the harsh tenets of Calvinism, declared that the divine principle of benevolence was dominant in man. Others, like Swift, oppressively aware of human perversity and irrationality, held fast to the doctrine of original sin or to something not far from it. Locke had begun to question the concept of a rational behavioral norm the observance of which was every man's moral obligation, and to attribute abnormal—that is, irrational—behavior to psychological disturbances beyond the control of the individual. Opinion was divided as to what lay ahead for the civilization then in being; the idea of progress was in process of formulation, but optimistic trends of thought were held in check by the widely felt fear that as the civilization which the Roman Empire had brought to the ancient world had finally gone down in ruins so could the ordered society that England then enjoyed.

Yet there was nothing in this scene that bespoke the kind of wrenching discord that leads to profound social disruption. The stabilizing factors were too strong; Augustan society was too deeply fixed in the experience of the generations preceding.

4

The Augustan period and the English Enlightenment as a whole lie open to many substantially different approaches. The one that the general reading public is probably most familiar with is that which lies through the literature of the time. There is the historical approach; J. H. Plumb's *Growth of Political Stability in England: 1675-1724,* previously referred to, is a first-rate example of what the modern historian is able, through a closer survey of the facts, to contribute to our better understanding of the political situation during the earlier Augustan period. Intellectual history—the historical study of the rise, spread, and mutation of ideas—has given and continues to give us new insights into Augustan thought. The work of present-day intellectual historians is sometimes concerned with individuals, sometimes with single concepts such as the idea of progress, or again with topics of a broad nature engaging many minds over an extended period, an example of the latter kind being S. A. Passmore's essay "The Malleability of Man in Eighteenth-Century Thoughts" (in

Aspects of the Eighteenth Century, ed. Earl R. Wasserman [1965]).

One of the newer approaches is the sociological. Two helpful commentaries on what the sociological consideration of literature entails and on some of the problems it presents are the study by Diana T. Laurenson and Alan Swingewood, *The Sociology of Literature* (1972), and Malcolm Bradbury's essay "Literature and Sociology" (in *Essays and Studies by Members of the English Association* [1970]). In what light Augustan authors will eventually be placed as a result of further inquiries of a sociological kind remains to be seen. J. H. Plumb's "The Public, Literature and the Arts in the 18th Century" (in *The Triumph of Culture: 18th Century Perspectives,* ed. Paul Fritz and David Williams [1972]) suggests how our point of view will perhaps be modified. There have been frequent attempts to devise a general theory that would account for the development of English culture since the Renaissance in terms of the steadily increasing importance of the middle class. The results, however, interesting as they are, have left many critics unconvinced, and in Diana Spearman's *The Novel and Society* (1966) we have a vigorous and compelling critique of the effort to interpret the eighteenth-century novel in England as a middle-class phenomenon. The theory urged on us by Ian Watt a few years ago in his "Two Historical Aspects of the Augustan Tradition," an essay given in *Studies in the Eighteenth Century: The David Nichol Smith Memorial Seminar, 1966* (1968), is an essentially different one, in that the political and social nature of English society during the Enlightenment is attributed not to the middle class but to the dominant influence of the landed interest, in the ascendant from 1640 onwards. Watt seeks to enforce his view by showing through many detailed references to Augustan literature how the writing of the period gave expression to the central concerns of the propertied class.

Each of these approaches has its own contribution to make. We know that the entire truth about any era of civilization must forever elude us; we can hope to discern only a portion of this truth, only certain segments of it. Yet this recognition of the indeterminable nature of a past era brings with it a heightened sense of the vital energies that informed it.

The present study does not represent a commitment to any procedural mode that can claim a distinctive name. It merely reflects an attitude now shared by many who feel that when a cultural period is approached primarily through individual figures of the time who in one way or another achieved memorable significance, the resulting perspective is a better one than any which reliance largely on our standard generalizations can yield. The position thus prompted is a mediating one between the individual and his age as the latter is conceived of in generic terms. The two, it is agreed, bear an inescapable relationship to one another. Only when the individual is seen bearing the coloration bestowed by the cultural period into which he was born can a genuinely fruitful study be pursued. But though recognized generalizations do indispensable service here, they are being put to the test. Do they stand up in the light of what is found to hold for the specific figures in question? Enforcement, modification if not total rejection—both are possible consequences of such an approach as this.

John Locke

Augustan Perspectives
Old and New

1 Locke over the Years

I f his reputation has suffered a decline in recent years, Locke still retains the historical importance that tradition has conferred on him. No one disputes the fact that in more ways than one he was the spokesman of his age—the new age of English liberalism ushered in by the Bloodless Revolution of 1688. Few at that time moulded public opinion to a similar extent; in work after work he caught the animating spirit of the post-Revolution years and gave it classic statement. The justification of the Revolution that he offered, his exposition of the principles basic to limited monarchy as at last established in England, his views on education—they are part of the Augustan structure of beliefs and accepted values. Above all, he was the father of British empiricism. We scarcely need to remind ourselves that the image he projected remained in clear view throughout the eighteenth century not only in England but in France and America as well.

We are likewise aware that his influence extended in precise ways through many specific areas. In the field of English letters, for instance, this influence was widespread and has been traced in detail.[1] Addison in his series of essays on the artistic imagination in *The Spectator* drew on Locke, as did Akenside in his widely read poem *The Pleasures of Imagination* and Thomson in *The Seasons;* in his *Analogy of Religion* Bishop Joseph Butler gave the theology of the period a new orientation that was Lockean in character; Gray once thought of turning the *Essay Concerning Human Knowledge* into a Latin poem; and Laurence Sterne,[2] as we know, kept Locke in mind while exploring with a humour all his own the human consciousness.

Nevertheless, general interest in Locke himself is at low ebb today. He is not one of the Augustans who like Swift steadfastly refuses to be ignored. His personality strikes us as colorless and his prose—an effective one in its time—does not attract modern readers. Those aspects of his thought which have popularly attached themselves to his name and which once received such wide acceptance no longer possess the force they once did.[3] Yet paradoxically more is known about him today—about his life at Oxford and in the wider world of English affairs, and about his interests and his intellectual development—than at any time in the past. The Lovelace Collection, consisting of thousands of letters and miscellaneous manuscripts, was acquired by the Bodleian Library, Oxford, in 1947 and for the first time became available to scholars. In his biographical study appearing in 1957, Maurice Cranston made use both of materials in the Lovelace Collection and of recent scholarly work, and in consequence was able to give an account of Locke's life that supersedes all earlier ones in fullness and accuracy of detail. Certain of Locke's earlier writings on religion and politics found in the Lovelace Collection have now been given us in modern scholarly editions,[4] and these tell us much that was not previously known about Locke's intellectual preoccupations shortly after the Restoration. A "medical biography," containing an edition of the medical notes found in the journals he kept over a twenty-five year period ending in 1698, has shown how deep and how sustained his interest in medical problems was.[5] Highly specialized studies have been appearing in a steady stream, and there are collections of modern essays like the one edited by J. W. Yolton—*John Locke: Problems and Perspectives* (1969)—designed to bring us abreast of recent developments in Lockean research and criticism.

Yet it would appear that in spite of all this modern scholarship—and one has only to glance through a recent bibliography entitled "Forty Years of Work on John Locke (1929-1969)"[6] to gain some understanding of how extensive it has been—general interest in Locke has not been rekindled. Indeed, this systematic study of Locke has sometimes resulted in turning indifference towards him into downright aversion, for he has been shown to be altogether of the seventeenth century and in consequence one who was looking at human nature and the human enterprise from a point of view that was much more restrictive, far less liberal in the popular sense, than that of the eighteenth-century rationalists.[7] To some it comes as an unwelcome shock to discover that "reason" to him still retained an element of the older reference to divine order, divine law, and the divine commands mankind is subject to.

How Locke stands today with the specialists is a question. A biographer like Maurice Cranston obviously places a high value on Locke's achievement, emphasizing its many-sided character. Professional philosophers are still concerned with problems presented by his thought and continue to explore them in books addressed primarily to academic colleagues. J. D. Mabbott, however, in a recent and less-specialized study[8] that gives a rounded survey of Locke's thought, points out that contemporary movements in analytic and linguistic philosophy have caused some extremists to question whether Locke's philosophic work retains any relevance at all. Mabbott himself is not shaken in his belief that despite the frequent inconsistencies in his thought, Locke remains the unmistakable founder of English philosophy. Since the Lovelace papers turn out to have more bearing on moral and political thought than on epistemology, Mabbott feels that a balanced treatment of Locke must be directed not only at his theory of the understanding but equally at his moral and political views. This is as much as to say that anyone dismissing Locke solely on the grounds that his epistemology is outdated is overlooking the true range of his speculations.[9]

Locke, now "so out of favour with philosophers of great analytic rigour and so much a favorite of historians of philosophy and ideas." So wrote the late Rosalie Colie, a perceptive commentator on Locke as a writer and man of letters, in one of her last essays.[10] And it can be said that it is

the intellectual historians rather than the philosophers proper—for whom the history of ideas as distinct from ideas *per se*
does not hold first place—who have been entering the strong-
est claims for Locke's central importance in the development
of modern culture. The claims are perhaps somewhat
exaggerated—as, for instance, those set forth in E. L. Tuveson's able though controversial study *The Imagination as a
Means of Grace: Locke and the Aesthetics of Romanticism* (1960)—
but they unquestionably deserve attention. According to another intellectual historian, G. S. Rousseau,[11] the imagination
was in a sense discovered in the late seventeenth century—the
imagination as a substantive reality, a material part of the
body capable of being described in physiological and medical
terms. It is to John Locke, Rousseau believes, that the literati
in England "owed more than to any other single man" their
knowledge of psychology.

Whether or not Locke's theory of the imagination was as
important a factor in the shaping of the eighteenth-century
Englishman's experience as some would have us believe, it
did hold unmistakable consequences for English literary art.
Under Locke's influence, men were led to think of reality less
as what lies in the world outside them and more as the
impressions taken by the imagination, and the subjective experience arising out of these impressions. Here we have the
immediate point of departure of that aesthetic movement
which in England during the decades following Locke's death
came to lay such stress upon the affective nature of poetry
and the other arts.

The new conception of the imagination likewise brought
with it decisive changes in the psychological approach to
human behavior, and in this respect, too, Locke's thinking,
though its effect was delayed, proved significant. Locke the
moralist hoped devoutly that men would prove capable,
through self-discipline, of conducting themselves according
to the dictates of reason, but he was forced to accept the fact
that human desires—the passions—often respond uncon-
trollably to the workings of the imagination, and he concluded that since this is in the nature of things, man is to be

regarded neither as innately good or bad but as an organism to be understood. His values, however, were not levelled by this kind of naturalism: a person's character, which is his characteristic behavior, could be moulded properly (the emphasis rests on "properly") while he was still young. Hence, for Locke, the paramount importance of sound education.

Now, it was nothing new to locate the source of the passions in the imagination. What was new was an attitude like Locke's, more scientific, less moralistic. More scientific meant among other things that the aberrations arising from the imagination were beginning to be seen as pathological and studied from a medical point of view. As madness became a disease alongside the long-recognized diseases affecting the body, the treatment of the insane underwent radical change. Here Locke is not to be credited with direct influence, but we see in certain passages in his medical notes how the spirit of the coming times was entering into his analysis of the malfunctions of the imagination. Madness, he wrote in his Journal late in 1677, seems to be a disorder in the imagination, not in the discursive faculty.[12] Some weeks later, in a longer and much more significant entry, he observed that madness consists not in the want of reason—granted their premises, madmen usually reason right—but in being controlled by the false ideas found in the imagination; but how imagination comes to have the power it does over men's minds he cannot guess; were it once known, "it would be no small advance towards the easier curing of this maladie."[13] Locke seemingly perceived two degrees of madness. We are all subject to the first degree, submitting partially and from time to time to the deceits of imagination; madmen, on the other hand, suffer from the second degree in that they are wholly under the control of these deceptions.

Locke's reputation as it once stood, his influence during the eighteenth century and beyond, and his reputation today among different groups distinguished from one another by their interests—such matters could, it goes without saying, be treated at infinitely greater length. What has just been set

forth serves to suggest, however, the diverse estimates of
Locke that have arisen over the years. But it seems possible to
aim at a somewhat different manner of assessment from any
of those noted above. To do so requires a much broader
approach than has commonly been taken—not to any one
facet of Locke's achievement, such as his political thought, or
his *Essay Concerning Human Understanding*, or his religious
writing, but to a man with a multiplicity of interests, culturally
and intellectually inheriting from the past more than he
perhaps fully realized, aware increasingly of the new perspectives that were opening up as the seventeenth century bur-
geoned to maturity, deeply involved,[14] sometimes to the point
of personal danger, in the political conflicts preceding the
great Revolution of 1688, searching always to understand the
nature of man and man's relationship to God. His ethics, his
psychology, his metaphysics, his sociopolitical views, his
theology are contradictory at many points, but behind all of
them a single personality is to be discerned, everlastingly
curious about the nature of things, ready to submit to the
findings of supposedly unprejudiced inquiry. Locke's influence, his meaning to others, is one thing; the man himself is
something else.

2   Locke's Life
A Résumé[15]

Born in 1632 and dying in 1704, Locke was destined to live
through seven decades of dramatic events in the life
of the nation and of challenging developments in the intellectual world. His father was a man of austerity and discipline; a
small Somerset landowner and clerk to local magistrates, he
had served with the Parliamentary forces during the Civil
War. Locke was fortunate in gaining admission to Westminster School, then presided over by the famous Richard Busby,
a confirmed royalist. In 1649, some months after Locke's
enrollment, Charles I was brought to execution at a site in

Whitehall not far from Westminster School. Three years later, when Locke went up to Christ Church, Oxford, on a scholarship, Cromwell assumed power. In due course Locke proceeded to the B.A. and the M.A. and was elected a Senior Student—the equivalent of Fellow—of Christ Church. Cromwell died a few months later. The Puritan regime was not long in coming to its sorry ending, and Charles II took the throne.

Locke had been changing with the times. As an undergraduate, responsive to his Puritan heritage and to the spirit of the period, he had written verse in praise of Cromwell. However, by 1660 he had become a monarchist through reasoned conviction. The disorders of the time had disturbed him profoundly. In a letter written in the autumn of 1659 he observed that imagination was "the great commander of the world"; "Phansye . . . rules us all under the title of reason"; it is our own passions, the brutish part of us, that govern our thoughts and actions; men's knowledge is nothing but opinion, opinion "moulded up betweene custome and Interest."[16] He was discovering the meaning of that middle way between extremes—the extremes in this instance of Royalist fanaticism and the blind enthusiasm of anti-Royalist Puritans—which only reason could make out and defend. It seems to have been more than a mere intellectual discovery. It was something deep inside—a conviction, a commitment, its consequences lifelong.

So began Locke's search for a reasonable and stable basis on which one's thought and conduct could rest. His early efforts to define such a basis are to be observed in two different series of writings, dating from the early 1660s but which remained unpublished until their recent appearance in two modern editions entitled *Two Tracts on Government* and *Essays on the Law of Nature*.[17] Unfortunately his discussion was set in terms that are so remote from what we are familiar with today that his actual position is easily misinterpreted as that of a reactionary. He had, it is true, welcomed the reestablished monarchy, but he had done so not because he had been won over to any belief in Divine Right but on grounds of historical precedent. And though he was as yet unable to accept the principle of religious toleration, through fear of the disorder that might ensue, in the course of a few years he was to change his position entirely in this respect. He had already been exposed to the sermons of John Owen, Dean of Christ Church during Locke's earlier years at Oxford and one of the earliest advocates of religious toleration. It was, however, in the course of a brief residence in Cleves, where he served during the winter of 1665-66 as secretary to a diplomatic mission to the Elector of Brandenberg and where he was enabled to observe toleration in actual practice, that the full meaning of this kind of religious freedom seems to have come home to him. Henceforth his belief in toleration, albeit in toleration with certain seemingly necessary restrictions, remained unshaken.

Locke the Oxford tutor is seen as a scholar alert to what was passing in the intellectual world, his outstanding characteristics being his deep moral concern together with his curiosity and openness of mind. At one point he considered taking orders in the Established Church, but for whatever reasons decided against such a course, and after his brief experience in the diplomatic service returned in 1666 to Oxford, where the new science was being enthusiastically taken up by a group of extraordinary men. The most distinguished of them was Robert Boyle, whose experiments with the air pump, leading to the formulation of Boyle's law, had established him as the foremost scientist of the day. Locke now associated himself with Boyle, and later, his interest having turned towards medicine, with Thomas Sydenham, the great English physician. Boyle and Sydenham were both in one sense children of Bacon in that they insisted upon an empirical approach to the natural phenomena they were investigating. In such an approach Locke found an answer to the problem posed by the confusions, uncertainties, and animosities arising from the world's opinions and dogmas. There was no more devout Christian than Boyle, but for him the natural order of the universe, though divinely established and maintained, was to be understood through empirical observation. Sydenham was equally emphatic in rejecting traditional interpretations in favor of actual, unprepossessed observation. Locke was profoundly influenced by such ideas. He was by this time a full-fledged "virtuoso"—one identified with the new experimental method and himself engaging in experiments and systematic observations, and sharing the hope of all Baconians for the advancement of man's estate through enhanced knowledge of the natural order. His studies extended to physics, meteorology, botany, and in particular, medicine—his medical notes, long and conscientiously kept, attest his sustained interest, and he was later to be granted the B.M. It is sometimes forgotten that by the standards of his time Locke was a qualified physician.

In 1667 Locke's life took an entirely new turn when he accepted the invitation extended by Lord Ashley—the two had met at Oxford—to take up residence with Ashley in London in the capacity of personal physician. As it turned out, Locke was to serve Ashley off and on until the latter's death sixteen years later. For Locke this was to prove a period of transcendent importance. Oxford was no backwater, but London was becoming the great intellectual focal center, attracting notable scientists—the recently established Royal Society held its meetings here at Gresham College—and clergymen of distinction as preachers and writers. Locke was able to pursue his scientific interests, being elected a fellow of the Royal Society, and with Sydenham beginning a book on clinical medicine. As a member of the congregation of St. Lawrence Jewry, in the City, he listened to the preaching of the vicar, Benjamin Whichcote, the notable Latitudinarian, who had once defined his aim as turning minds away from argumentation and words to the reason of things and to "the great moral and spiritual realities lying at the basis of all religion."[18] Locke the Latitudinarian, defending the principle of toleration and in religion seeking reason as the support of our beliefs, is to be placed within this environment of ideas. In his mind the empiricism of the new science and what Whichcote spoke of as "the inward of things" and "the reason of them" were now coming together.

It was his association with Ashley, however, that was preeminently important. Anthony Ashley Cooper, born in 1621, had achieved prominence in public affairs as a young man, and at the Restoration had taken office under Charles II, was raised to the peerage as Baron Ashley, and in 1672 was created first Earl of Shaftesbury and became Lord Chancellor. The question of Charles's successor now loomed large, and Shaftesbury took the lead in pushing for an Exclusion Bill the purpose of which was to keep Charles's brother James, a Roman Catholic, from the throne. Dismissed as Lord Chancellor, Shaftesbury set about organizing the opposition to the King and the royal policy. Thus the Whig party came into existence, Protestant to an extreme, favoring toleration for Dissenters, and looking to Parliament to check the power of the executive. Shaftesbury drove matters to a climax, which came in 1681 when Charles dismissed Parliament, and the government began a resolute drive against political dissidents. Shaftesbury was seized, charged with high treason, and committed to the Tower, but was eventually freed when a Grand Jury refused to indict him. A year afterwards, late in 1682, he fled to Holland, dying in Amsterdam a few months afterwards.

A strong bond of mutual understanding and respect seems to have existed between Locke and Shaftesbury. The latter, seriously ill in 1668, credited Locke with saving his life; the following year Locke arranged the marriage of Shaftesbury's eldest son, and later was in attendance at the birth of Shaftesbury's grandson, the future third Earl and philosophic writer. It was under Shaftesbury's influence that Locke became the great Whig theoretician. Undoubtedly Locke's socio-economic views were already firmly established when he joined Shaftesbury. His "liberalism" is to be seen as something essentially traditional to that entire class of Englishmen extending from people like his father, possessed of small but independent means, through the wealthy landed gentry: property was to them symbolic, and with it went constitutional freedoms, established in the past, that they were determined to uphold against the incursions of a central, executive power.

Nevertheless, Locke's service under Shaftesbury, who has been described by Maurice Cranston as "the complete progressive capitalist in politics," confirmed and strengthened Locke's inherited bent. In the course of his first months with Shaftesbury, Locke prepared a reasoned statement in support of toleration. This statement not only served as the basis of a memorial which Shaftesbury presented to the king, but it contained in substance much of what over twenty years later was to constitute Locke's famous *Letters Concerning Toleration*.

During a period of over three years Locke was living in France, but in 1679 he returned home, apparently at Shaftesbury's request. National affairs were now moving towards a crisis, with Shaftesbury and his followers pitted against the king and demanding a constitutional change that would have excluded James from the throne. Shaftesbury stood in need of reinforcement in the way of articulated theory. There is reason to believe that Locke's *Two Treatises of Government*, first published in 1690 and received, as they were then intended to be, as a statement of the principles which the Revolution had just confirmed, go back in substance to what Locke had previously worked out for Shaftesbury and so were originally called forth by events of the 1679-81 period.

With Shaftesbury's fall Locke was left in an exposed position, watched by the authorities and perhaps in some personal danger. The great things governing men are, he wrote in his Journal, reason, passion, and superstition; the first, he continued, "governs a few, the two last share the bulk of mankind and possess them in their turns. But superstition most powerfully produces the greatest mischief."[19] Before long Shaftesbury was dead. In England there were underground movements and plots. All that is known concerning Locke is that by early September 1683 he was in Rotterdam, a refugee with other fellow countrymen of like persuasion.

The period of his life that had now come to an end, the period comprising his years with Shaftesbury, had been one of remarkable intellectual activity on his part. He had carried on his studies in science and medicine; he had addressed himself to some of the most urgent problems of the times—to the question of toleration, to economic policy, to political theory. And it was then that he had first turned to philosophy in earnest. In the "Epistle to the Reader," which stands as an introduction to the *Essay Concerning Human Understanding,* Locke tells of the circumstances that started him on his philosophic explorations. In the course of a discussion which he and some of his friends were engaged in "they found themselves . . . quickly at a stand." It then occurred to him that they were on the wrong course. Before setting themselves upon inquiries of such a nature, it was necessary to examine their own abilities, and see what "*objects* [their] understandings were, or were not, fitted to deal with." Locke does not date this episode, which apparently occurred sometime in the winter of 1671-72, nor does he indicate the precise subject under discussion, though fortunately one of the friends who were present was to record that it concerned "principles of morality and revealed religion."[20] By the summer of 1671 he had made an early draft of the *Essay,* and this he had re-worked in an enlarged form by the end of the year. It was not until the 1680s, after he had taken refuge in Holland, that he managed to complete his *Essay,* a summary of which appeared in French in the *Bibliothèque universelle* in 1688, some two years before its English publication. For those who find in Locke a significance extending beyond his formal philosophical work, and who see him in broad, humanistic terms as one deeply engaged in the life around him and searching constantly for the reason of things—for such the importance of the *Essay* will rest less in what it stands for in the history of empiricism *per se* than in its approach to those "principles of morality and revealed religion" wherein he and his friends had once found themselves at a stand.

Locke's exile lasted for more than five years, during which time he lived in a variety of places, first at Amsterdam and latterly at Rotterdam. The situation in England was brought home to him in more ways than one. In 1684 he was expelled from his Christ Church studentship, and a year later, at the time of the Monmouth rebellion, the English authorities sought his extradition and for some months he went into hiding, at one time under the assumed name of Dr. van der Linden. Nor, until unmistakable signs began to signal the coming of a new order in England, was there a forseeable end to his exile.

There could not have been many moments free from apprehensions, yet he was able to pursue, with fewer distractions now, his varied intellectual interests. Making new friends, meeting and conversing with interesting people, travelling extensively through the Dutch republic, he established himself as a recognized member of the free intellectual community that then sheltered in Holland. He read widely—in travel books, from which he gained an enlarged awareness of human ways, and in learned publications of the sort that he was called upon to review in the pages of the *Bibliothèque universelle*. His interest in medical matters did not lapse entirely, but throughout his stay in Holland he was largely taken up with philosophy, with educational theory, and with problems of religious belief and religious toleration.

His Latitudinarian persuasions were already firmly settled; the atmosphere of religious freedom which prevailed in Holland and the contrast with things in England were cause both for rejoicing and sorrowing. Two of his new friends in Holland appear to have added breadth and depth to his religious convictions. Philip van Limborch was a professor of theology at the Remonstrants' seminary in Amsterdam; his religious views, like those of his fellow Remonstrants, defined a position similar to that of the English Latitudinarians, the emphasis resting on moral conduct, rational assent to a few simple scriptural truths, and toleration. It was to Limborch that Locke originally addressed his *Letter Concerning Toleration,* written in 1686 (though it stemmed from the position papers he had previously prepared for Shaftesbury) and published first in Latin and then in English in 1689, a second *Letter* following in 1690, a third in 1692. The other friend was Benjamin Furley, a Quaker, in whose house at Rotterdam Locke lived as a paying guest during his last two years in Holland. Locke did not withdraw from the Church of England, but his sense of true Christian fellowship was not governed by church membership; Remonstrants and Quakers no less than he sought "the inwards of things" and "the reason of them."

If the *Letter Concerning Toleration* is not philosophy in the close sense, it was a philosopher who wrote it. The *Essay Concerning Human Understanding* had been steadily taking shape since Locke came to Holland; in September 1686 he was sending the third book back to friends in England to examine, and then on the last day of that year he finished the work, an epitome of which appeared in 1688 in the *Bibliothèque universelle*. It is important, when considering what the *Essay* reveals about Locke himself, to take into account those elements in the work which can easily be glossed over if attention is focused too narrowly upon what the textbooks point to as Lockian empiricism. The drive behind the entire work was his determination to set in proper terms our knowledge of the inwards of things—what we could know of the Divine, and the means at our disposal. His thoughts on toleration carry with them the implications of the *Essay;* it was not a matter of chance that the composition of the *Letter Concerning Toleration* overlapped that of his chief philosophic work.

One would be unjustified in suggesting that the writings of these years spent in Holland were conceived as variant expressions of a central ideological theme; Locke was an occasional writer in the sense that each piece of his grew out of a particular situation or set of problems. Yet this having been said, it is only right to add that although his compositions do not fit together to make an insistently unified whole they are not out of accord with one another. And as the *Essay* and the *Letter Concerning Toleration* evidence the same intuition, so do the *Essay* and Locke's famous treatise on education, most of which derives from the period of exile. *Some Thoughts Concerning Education,* which first appeared in 1693, originated in a series of letters addressed to Edward Clarke, an old Somerset friend, concerning the education of Clarke's son. Though the book excited less interest among Locke's contemporaries than did other writings of his, before the end of the eighteenth century it had become a major influence in modern theories

of education. A long line of educational commentators—
Milton being the most famous—had preceded Locke, and his
prescriptions concerning the subjects to be taught and
methods of instruction were not arrestingly novel. What distinguishes *Some Thoughts* and gives it the great importance it
has enjoyed among liberal educationalists is the theory of
human development that it carries with it. The individual is
innately neither good nor bad, and since early impressions
and early influences more than anything else determine his
character as a mature person, proper education is of supreme
importance. Were there no incorrigible beings, no uncontrollable passions within the human psyche? Locke did not
deny that there were, but Locke the optimist managed to keep
intact his faith that men were nevertheless capable of reason.

Early in February 1689 Locke returned to England. He was
then fifty-six, and though he had earned the confidence and
respect of many of the prominent persons now coming into
power, and was not unknown in learned circles on the Continent, he had published nothing of consequence. In a matter
of months, however, three of his most important works now
appeared—the *Letter Concerning Toleration, Two Treatises of
Government,* and the *Essay,* all on sale before the close of
1689[21]—and although he then acknowledged only the *Essay,*
his identity was firmly established; by the mid-nineties he had
become as much of a national figure as Isaac Newton.

More publications followed: in 1690 a second *Letter Concerning Toleration,* a third two years later; in 1693 *Some Thoughts
Concerning Education,* subsequently enlarged; in 1694 the second edition of the *Essay,* and in 1700 the fourth edition, which
added to Book IV the important nineteenth chapter, "Of
Enthusiasm"; in 1695 *The Reasonableness of Christianity as Delivered in the Scriptures.* The Revolution had brought an end to
civil warfare but not to warfare in the press, and Locke was
caught up in controversy with some of the writers who were
attacking him, one for his declared position on toleration,
another for the views set forth in *The Reasonableness of Christianity,* and a third, no less a dignitary than Edward Stillingfleet, Bishop of Worcester, for imputed heterodoxy in the

Essay. Locke felt compelled to defend himself, and his responses—three were addressed to Stillingfleet—appeared at intervals throughout the nineties.

These publications were not, however, the exclusive center of his activities from 1689 onwards. One of the things that distinguished the earlier period of the English Enlightenment—roughly, the half-century following the Revolution—was the participation of so many of its writers in public affairs. Swift, satirist for all times, was likewise a Tory propagandist; Bolingbroke, the would-be philosopher, had been one of Queen Anne's chief ministers; Addison the essayist, commentator on Augustan mores and Lockian aesthetics, was a Commissioner for Trade and served briefly as one of the Secretaries of State. Locke, having seen Shaftesburian political concepts translated into fact by the Revolution, and having by means of the *Two Treatises of Government* brought myth, as it were, to the support of fact, was accorded an active role in national affairs. Shortly after his return to England he was offered the post of Ambassador to the Elector of Brandenburg; this he refused, accepting instead a minor appointment as a Commissioner of Appeals. How highly he was regarded by those in power was shown clearly when in the autumn of 1689 John Somers, the eminent Whig statesman and future Lord Chancellor, sought his advice. He and Newton now met, Locke having already acknowledged the achievement of his great contemporary by his reference in the *Essay* to "the incomparable Mr. Newton."

Locke was suffering from chronic asthma but in 1696, in spite of his physical difficulties, he accepted an appointment to the newly created Board of Trade, and as one of the Commissioners of Trade served with great energy for four years. It need not surprise us that the policies he advocated as a commissioner reflected the social and economic beliefs deeply ingrained in the English governing classes. It went without question, for instance, that England could allow no economic competition from Ireland, and Locke was at one with his fellow members of the Board of Trade regarding measures necessary to restrict Irish woolen manufactures, seen only as a threat to English industry. When the board approached the perennial problems of unemployment and the most effective ways of dealing with the indigent, Locke submitted a paper[22] in which he set forth in much detail his own scheme for dealing with poverty and unemployment. These proposals of his failed, it is true, to receive the backing of his colleagues on the board, but despite what seems to us the unconscionable severity of his recommendations, the attitude they expressed was one undoubtedly shared by many at that time. The poor multiply, Locke observes, and taxes for their maintenance increase. This evil arises neither from scarcity of provision nor want of employment, for "the goodness of God has blessed these times with plenty "; the growth of the poor has as a cause "nothing else but the relaxation of discipline and corruption of manners," vice and idleness going together. In order to restrain the debauchery of the poor, superfluous brandy shops and unnecessary ale-houses should be suppressed; vagabonds found begging outside their own parishes should be put aboard ships of the royal navy to serve three years at soldier's pay, and under severe circumstances should lose their ears or be transported as in the case of felons; and children of laboring people, ordinarily a burden to the parish, should be placed, between the ages of three and fourteen, in working schools to be set up in every parish.[23]

It was in the midst of his labors as a commissioner that Locke undertook to write an additional chapter for insertion in the *Essay. Of the Conduct of the Understanding,* as he called his work, remained unfinished and appeared for the first time, in his *Posthumous Works,* two years after his death. It is the most readable of all his philosophic works, and for the general reader the best introduction there is to the essential Locke, the empiricist and at the same time and in his own way the undeterred rationalist.

Another post, presumably a diplomatic one, was now urged upon Locke by the King, but Locke declined it. His health was visibly failing, and in 1700 he resigned from the Board of Trade. His last years were spent, when not in London, mostly

at Oates, in Essex, as the paying guest of Sir Francis and Lady
Masham—the latter, the daughter of the Cambridge Platonist
Ralph Cudworth, a longtime and dearly regarded friend.
Some of his time was devoted to studying the Epistles of St.
Paul and to writing the paraphrase and notes which were
published shortly after his death. There were meetings with
new and old friends, one of the new being Anthony Collins,
future author of the *Discourse of Freethinking,* the deistic book
which was to call forth among other attacks Swift's ironic *Mr.
Collins's Discourse of Freethinking.* Collins was a profound ad-
mirer of Locke's and was warmly received at Oates. There is
no reason to believe, however, that Locke would ever have
given his approval to the *Discourse* and Collins's subsequent
works.

Death was now approaching. Locke faced it with compo-
sure, as is apparent from the magnificent portrait by Sir
Godfrey Kneller done at Oates in the late summer of 1704.
On October 28 of that year the end came. Locke had prepared his own epitaph, in which he described himself as one
content with his place in life, brought up as a scholar and
devoting his work wholly to the search for truth.

Locke never warns us. He does not ask us for our sympathy. He bids us join him in what he saw as the noblest of all
endeavors, the search for truth.

3   Locke's Thought
An Informal Commentary

W hen we speak of Locke's philosophy[24] we usually have
in mind the concepts placed before us in the *Essay
Concerning Human Understanding.* Locke's approach to epistemology is well known. There are no inherent notions, principles, ideas stamped upon the mind of man—so we are told at
the start of the *Essay.* On the contrary, all we have in the way of
knowledge is attained entirely by the use of our natural faculties. Book I of the *Essay* consists of an attack—an almost impas-

sioned one—on the theory that men bring with them into the world certain ideas. In his opening chapter Locke pauses long enough to give us the gist of his own theory, counter to the one under attack: the mind is as it were an empty cabinet, into which the senses introduce particular ideas.

In developing his theory of knowledge in the further course of the *Essay,* Locke points to the ideas originating in sense and to the further ideas that result from the operation of our minds in what we call reflection. Knowledge—all knowledge—is said to lie "in the perception of the agreement or disagreement of any of our ideas." There are, however, different sorts of knowledge. "Intuitive knowledge" arises from an immediate and instinctive comparing of any two ideas. "Sensitive knowledge" reaches "no further than the existence of things actually present to our senses." And there is what Locke designates as "rational knowledge"; here the coherence or incoherence of our ideas is perceived through a process of rational discourse—or reasoning, that is; of reason in action.

Locke's confidence in the power of human reason is great, and it is this confidence that points to a kind of rationalism which his basic empiricism entails. For Locke, reason is not an eternal, universal principle embracing all Being; it is an instrument, a God-given faculty—"that faculty whereby man is supposed to be distinguished from beasts, and wherein it is evident he much surpasses them." However, reason has its limits; it can give us true knowledge only out of such ideas as may be present in the mind. Man faces a natural universe much of which lies and will always lie beyond his comprehension.

In the fourth and concluding book of the *Essay* Locke comes to the questions which for him are all-important and which from the outset he has had in mind: how is man's understanding, operating with the ideas which the mind has attained, able in some instances to arrive at certain knowledge, in others only at probability? Above all, what is the relationship between the human understanding and our religious faith?

But the *Essay,* despite its importance, does not give us an

adequate conception of Locke's thought in its broad range
and multiplicity of intentions. His philosophy in the narrow
sense is his empirical theory of knowledge, and it is with this
that so many of the professional philosophers who have given
us studies of Locke have understandably enough been preoc-
cupied. However, as Peter Laslett among others has re-
minded us,[25] Locke did not confine himself to epistemology.
He also wrote on political theory, on toleration, on economics,
on education, on religion. And not everything fits together.
Evident are certain discrepancies and gaps. Yet we are always
conscious of the presence of John Locke. His thought is a
distinctive attitude; it does not constitute a closed, coordinate
system. Efforts have been made to show that there are unify-
ing threads running through all his works, but the results are
not completely convincing. Locke's peculiar mark and his
peculiar virtue is that he moves from occasion to occasion,
accepting each confronting situation as a thing given and to
be newly searched. The "historical, plain method" he speaks
of in the Introduction to the *Essay*, the method he will use in
inquiring into the human understanding, describes his cus-
tomary approach—"historical" in that it takes that which is
inviting study as a concrete reality here and now, "plain"
because its tools are what everyday experience provides us
with.

Many different approaches to Locke's thought suggest
themselves. The one taken here is essentially historical in that
it seeks to relate Locke to some of the outstanding problems
of his time involving intellectual theories, political and social
values, and matters of religion and ethics. The ways in which
he responded point clearly, it is believed, to significant forces
present in his thought.

We may begin by looking at the manner in which he shows
the influence of the kind of English Protestantism associated
in the seventeenth century with the Established Church. On
the one hand there were the enthusiasts, acknowledging only
the promptings of their emotional experience; on the other
were the Roman Catholics, whose faith, it was constantly
charged, rested solely on unquestioning acceptance of an

unreasoning authority. Anglicans turned away from both of these extremes, seeking instead what they frequently referred to as the *via media*. The middle way was essentially Protestant in spirit; the individual stood face to face with God—with God as he revealed Himself in Holy Writ—and one's acceptance of God through his Word was a thing authorized by reason. Faith was not reason, but man was intended to reason about his faith. A reasonable faith meant that the grounds of one's belief were such as could be validated through a process of rational discourse. This we may call a kind of rationalism if we choose, but it is clearly not rationalism of a sort to inflate man's pride, for human knowledge, though sufficient for our purposes on earth, is limited in kind and in range.

The extent to which Locke's theory of knowledge reflects the spirit of the Anglican *via media* and its basic pattern has not always been appreciated. Locke's aversion to enthusiasm, which he associates primarily with enthusiasm in religion, is expressed time and again, and most prominently in Chapter XIX of Book IV of the *Essay*, where it is characterized as the laying aside of reason and the wish to set up revelation without it. His rejection of Roman Catholicism was such that in his *Letter Concerning Toleration* he denied to its adherents the right to be tolerated by the civil magistrate. His was a rational faith, embodying that relationship between faith and reason that is marked out in such insistent detail in one of the climactic chapters of the *Essay*—Chapter XVIII of Book IV—entitled "Of Faith and Reason, and their Distinct Provinces." Here we see how Locke's philosophic theory of knowledge and his Anglican rationalism proceed side by side.

It is, however, with the European intellectual revolution of the seventeenth century that Locke has most frequently been associated. That he was profoundly affected by this portentous shift in orientation goes without saying. As Milton at Cambridge came to hate the old scholasticism, so did Locke as a student at Oxford, and his later attack in the *Essay* on innate ideas is the ultimate expression of his steadfast refusal from his formative years onwards to accept traditional formularies in philosophic matters. The new astronomy, the new physics, and the new mathematics were revealing a different kind of physical universe; increasingly the traditional concepts regarding the entire natural order of things were being called in question. Descartes' dualism, separating the mind with its rational powers from the natural universe lying outside the mind, raised in a crucial manner the problem of man's knowledge of the external world: what could be known of it, and by what process?

Apparently it was only on the eve of his departure from Oxford for service under Shaftesbury that Locke began to read Descartes. It must have been with much excitement that he perceived how Cartesianism, in facing up to the recent developments in Continental science, gave rise through its dualism of mind and matter to new problems concerning man's knowledge of the reality outside the mind, and the actual nature of that reality. But the Cartesian system was not for Locke. It did indeed pose epistemological questions in a way that could not be disregarded, but it dealt with such questions in terms of a deductive rationalism that was wholly foreign to him. He had already been exposed to the empirical, inductive approach favored by many in England, as by his two friends, Boyle the chemist and Sydenham the physician, both of whom demonstrated in their own scientific work the effectiveness of the experimental method.

However, it was not solely under the influence of English experimental science that Locke turned towards the empiricism with which he has been associated ever since the publication of the *Essay Concerning Human Understanding*. His whole bent was entirely against any form of the dogmatic. Just as there were few things in religion that were to be accepted on authority, so in philosophy and science there was little that could stand by virtue of rationalistic theorizing. The human self faced a world of nature, known insofar as it *was* known through sense data interpreted by our faculty of understanding. One must learn to be content with probable knowledge, in the meantime continuing with all the energy at one's command the presumably endless search for truth, a spiritual as well as an intellectual adventure.

Locke would not have developed as he did either in philosophy or in his political and social thinking had he not so fully committed himself to the principle of religious toleration. He had experienced toleration in action while at Cleves in the winter of 1665-66; at Oxford he had witnessed men like John Owen leading the reaction against the religious dogmatisms that had been setting Englishmen so fiercely against one another; and when he joined Shaftesbury he not only associated himself with an ardent spokesman for toleration but found Latitudinarianism being ably espoused by London clergymen of eminence. Locke was at one with the Latitudinarians in his hope that religious differences of a seemingly nonessential kind—differences which, it was held, did not touch the central points of faith—might be composed, or at least that they might no longer be insisted upon in ways that split apart the Christian community. We can have no precise appreciation, he felt, of another man's relationship with God; therefore let us not pass judgement upon his religious experience, let us not attach to him any devisive terms or refuse him toleration.

This generosity of spirit and openmindedness is heartwarming indeed. In his efforts on behalf of religious toleration he is at his finest, contrasting with those Augustans who, despite the Toleration Act of 1689, which at long last had lifted from Dissenters the penalties imposed on them in Charles II's time, sustained a degree of hostility towards Protestant nonconformists. Here Locke's goodwill is beyond question, but what are we to say of his implied judgment of human nature and the human situation? His hope—his assumption, indeed—that in the disputes and mutual animosities arising out of differences of belief, reasonableness can in the end prevail, rests on a psychology of human behavior that would appear to take into account only conscious, reasoning factors. It is only fair to point out that his hope had in a measure been borne out by contemporary historical events. The Revolution and the accompanying Toleration Act must have seemed to him triumphs of political-social reasonableness which had come to pass almost miraculously after years during which unreason appeared unchallengeable.

The question remains, however, whether Locke was blind
to the nonrational factors, to our emotional sets, to the dark
forces operating in the unconscious, and the best answer that
we can give is that sometimes he was indeed blind, whereas at
other times he showed an acute awareness of the irrational
elements present in us all. From the first, he recognized in
religious enthusiasm a standing threat to common sense.
Here he is to be associated with a whole line of seventeenth-
century writers who assailed enthusiasm in religion unremittingly. The attack was made in the name of reason, and
Locke's position in the chapter "Of Enthusiasm," which in the
fourth edition of the *Essay* he added to Book IV, is, in this
sense, a rationalistic one: enthusiasm, "rising from the conceits of a warmed or overweening brain," sets reason aside.
And as a physician observing the insane he had previously, in
an entry made in his Journal in 1677, noted that "Madnesse
seems to be noething but a disorder in the imagination, and
not in the discursive faculty."[26] In another entry made a few
weeks later he remarked that the ideas stored in the memory
are ideas of things we have observed to exist, whereas the
imagination yields "a picture drawne in our mind without
reference to a patterne"; furthermore, disordered imagination affects not only madmen but others who "think long and
intently upon one thing" and so "come at last to have their
minds disturbed about it and to be a little cracked as to that
particular."[27] How this disorder comes about Locke here con-
fessed that he could not guess, but as a means of checking
extraordinary flights of the imagination he recommended
"haveing often recourse to ones memory and tieing downe
the minde strictly to the recollecting things past precisely as
they were." Reason in the Lockean sense—"the perception of
the agreement and disagreement of any of our ideas"—can
and should assert its power to regulate our conduct.

Yet there were times when Locke's confidence that the
sanity conferred by reason was strong enough to govern our
warm and overweening conceits was checked by a somewhat
altered view of the imagination. What was the line separating
clinical madness from the irrational experience we all are

subject to in one degree or another? Locke came to this problem in Chapter XXXIII of the second book of the *Essay,* another of the chapters added to the fourth edition. In what he called "the association of ideas" he perceived an operative factor in the human psyche which seemed to undercut the sovereign role of the conscious understanding: we observe something unreasonable in most men, who in many cases are unwilling to yield to the evidence of reason; such opposition to reason deserves the name of madness, and in fact "there is scarce a man so free from [the kind of behaviour], but that if he should always, on all occasions, argue or do as in some cases he constantly does, would not be thought fitter for Bedlam than civil conversation." There is, in short, "a degree of madness found in most men." Madness of this sort is to be traced to the wrong connection of ideas made by custom, and such "wrong and unnatural combination of ideas" will be found "to establish the irreconcilable opposition between different sects of philosophy and religion."

It is to be noted that Locke termed the combination of ideas he was discussing as "wrong and unnatural." Wrong they unquestionably were in that they misrepresented and misinterpreted, and in this sense they were similarly unnatural, yielding conclusions contrary to the right order of things. But, to shift the point of reference from the world outside us to the world of inner experience, these irrational combinations of ideas could scarcely be called unnatural since they were actual, observed occurrences. Involved here is the distinction between "Nature," a nominative and hence excluding concept, and all-embracing "nature." Locke was leaning in the direction of "nature" when in the course of this same chapter he wrote that when a wrong combination of ideas has been established and as long as it lasts, "it is not in the power of reason to help us, and relieve us from the effects of it. Ideas in our minds, when they are there, will operate according to their natures and circumstances." Hence there is emerging that new view of the imagination referred to in the opening section above—a view betokening, according to one intellectual historian, the virtual discovery of the imagination as a part of the body, and subject like the rest of the body to material description and medical treatment. The gap between madness and everyday behavior was closing; Nature was giving way to the natural.

But in Locke's case it was his vision of sanity that prevailed. Reason was always there to mark for us the course of common sense, and reason was a powerful persuader if not always an irresistible one. He never, like Swift, glimpsed the terrifying spectre of a world completely and perpetually in a state of madness. To some degree Locke's expectation of sanity was a temperamental matter, but it was one he shared with others of his time, notably Latitudinarians and all the advocates of religion toleration.

There was a time when any commentary on Locke's political thought would have begun and perhaps ended with reflections upon his *Two Treatises of Government.* This is scarcely the case today. As we now know, the two essays are not to be referred exclusively to events associated with the Revolution of 1689. Locke apparently began them a decade before the Revolution, at the time when Shaftesbury's challenge to royal authority was approaching a climax. He was then pleading a cause as yet in jeopardy, and he aimed at rhetorical effectiveness. Later, in preparing for the publication in 1690 of the *Two Treatises,* he undoubtedly revised his earlier work and perhaps extended it. His discussion was thus brought into accord with the electrifying events of the preceding months, but its original character, essentially rhetorical in that it was above all designed to persuade, remained unchanged.

This is not to say that the political theory expounded in the *Treatises*—the second *Treatise* is here the important one—was in any way a specious thing, advanced by Locke not because it expressed views which he genuinely held but rather as an effective stratagem lending support to an essentially political cause. We are taken back to man's original, "natural" state—"a state . . . of equality, wherein all the power and jurisdiction is reciprocal."[28] This state of nature "has a law of nature to govern it." This law, which is "reason," obliges everyone, and teaches all mankind "that, being all equal and independent, no one ought to harm another in his life, health, liberty, or possessions." Yet there are inconveniences in this state of nature, to remedy which a government is established. Such a government comes into being through the consent of the individuals comprising the community, each person agreeing to give up such of his natural power as is necessary to the end for which he and his fellows have united in society. But it is not an absolute government, its whole purpose being to safeguard man's natural rights—his life, liberty, health, body, and above all his property—but to do so under established law:

> ... freedom of men under government is to have a standing rule to live by, common to every one of that society, and made by the legislative power erected in it; a liberty to follow my own will in all things, where that rule prescribes not; and not to be subject to the inconstant, uncertain, unknown, arbitrary will of another man: as freedom of nature is to be under no other restraint but the law of nature.[29]

It is a statement, all this, that stands against the rich background of western political thought extending from classical times down through England's troubled seventeenth century, with its Thomas Hobbes and a number of lesser English writers on the theory of government. The concept of natural law, which lies at the center of Locke's discussion, was nothing new. What Locke did when originally seeking to give support to Shaftesbury was to use this concept in order to confer plausibility and authority on the Whig struggle against Charles II's exercise of an overriding executive power. But by the turn of historical events, the natural law proclaimed in the second *Treatise* became in 1690 the justification of that political-social order established at the Revolution, and long continued to give an almost absolute authority to the principles and workings of the liberal order of society in both Great Britain and America.

Three points may be made apropos of the *Treatises*. The

first, which has perhaps been stressed sufficiently already, is that Locke adopted a manner of writing aimed at persuading his readers. This, however, may be added. Though the modern reader may regard it as farfetched that anything of Locke's could be termed rhetorical, a careful analysis which has been made of the style of the second *Treatise*[30] has shown convincingly that Locke has frequently resorted to reasoning which is more rhetorical in character than strictly logical. Yet he was entirely sincere. Distortion, let alone downright misinterpretation—these, we may believe, were farthest from his thoughts, and as things turned out, he had provided liberalism with a supporting myth of great cogency—a myth which so long as it worked must be regarded as possessing a degree of validity.

Secondly, though Locke's "law of nature" is such a key factor in the political theory that emerges from the *Treatises,* it is not clearly established there, nor can it easily be made to accord with the *Essay's* vehement rejection of innate ideas. Those who read Locke with any care are repeatedly made aware that his thought is not a closed, carefully integrated system; there are unexplained things, and the treatment of certain topics is sometimes such as to leave us confused. From early on in his intellectual career Locke involved himself with the concepts which the thinkers of the period were attaching to law—natural law, divine law, civil law—but the course of his thinking on the subject is not easily followed.[31] By the time he arrived at the *Essay* he was declaring that although "a great part of mankind give testimony to the law of nature," moral rules cannot be innate nor "so much as self-evident." We are led to conclude—and perhaps this is enough to say—that the confidence with which natural law is advanced in the *Treatises* is not reflected uniformly throughout his writings.

The third point is the most important one. It is concerned, not with what has found its way into the *Treatises,* but with the things which have not. In presenting his view of rational freedom and the kind of political arrangements that would ensure such freedom, Locke has eschewed actual historical examples. As Peter Laslett observes in his informative discussion included in his edition of the *Two Treatises*, there is nothing concerning the tradition of Canon Law, the English House of Commons, and the "ancient constitution." Those of Locke's precursors who had also pressed the case against an unchecked executive power had made much of these. Their omission by Locke may have been a calculated one, intended to shift the debate to what seemed a more effective level. But as a result we cannot afford to rest our consideration of Locke's political thought solely on the *Treatises*. His presuppositions, which are not expressed there, were the determining force. They were those of Englishmen of the propertied class, from men of some wealth down through small landowners like Locke's father. It was they who had been offering resistance in the House of Commons to the efforts of the Stuarts to centralize in the executive the power of the state, and it was their values—the values informing their social, economic, and political principles—that Locke embodied. His political liberalism is of the seventeenth century and in stressing as he did the right of property he was speaking for men of his own class, for the gentry, that is, enjoying an established place in the traditional social scheme and jealous of their inherited rights.

One cannot live with Locke for very long without becoming aware that in his thought there are revealed some areas of uncertainty. There are important questions that he answered somewhat differently at different times. His desire to find the truth about the condition of things remained unshaken, but in the course of his unfolding experience, both practical and intellectual, new perspectives presented themselves and previously established relationships seemed to call for modification.

It has already been pointed out in connection with his commitment to the principle of religious toleration that although his faith in reason—in human reasonableness, that is—never deserted him, he did not remain unaware that there were irrational forces present in man that posed a threat to commonsense behavior. The historical, plain approach to

man's basic nature presented problems that could not be
evaded but for which there were no ready solutions. Here is
the area within which occur the most obtrusive uncertainties
encountered by the reader of Locke. Is not order, social and
political, brought about and maintained by the exercise of
reason? Is not the freedom of the individual within our society likewise the consequence of our own rational behavior
towards one another? But *is* it all clear sailing? One recalls the
passage, previously referred to, which Locke entered in his
Journal in 1681:[32] "The three great things that govern mankind are reason, passions and superstition. The first governs a
few, the two last share the bulk of mankind and possess them
in their turns. But superstition most powerfully produces the
greatest mischief." This was written, to be sure, not long after
Charles II had dismissed the Oxford Parliament and effectively thwarted Shaftesbury's challenge; there was every immediate reason for Locke's pessimism. Yet this was by no
means the sole occasion when his faith in man as a reasonable
being was severely tried. In his *Reasonableness of Christianity,*
which appeared in 1695, we find a severe discrediting of
reason's role. Though God's reasonableness in his relations
with men is declared throughout this treatise, Locke is at the
same time asserting the insufficiency of human reason in the
moral realm: it is plain "that human reason unassisted failed
men in its great and proper business of morality. It never
from unquestionable principles, by clear deduction, made out
an entire body of the 'law of nature'." From this there follows
Locke's conclusion that salvation lies through belief in Christ
and in his and the apostles' preaching; Christ completes the
moral law laid upon us in the Old Testament, "giving its full
and clear sense, free from the corrupt and loosening glosses
of the scribes and pharisees."

Previous to this Locke had at one time seen in the Law of
Nature a code universally recognized among men and universally binding. At other times he questioned this universality.
In the *Essay* his position seems to have been that although we
are not endowed with any innate principles, we can discover
laws of morality and sufficient motives for obedience to them
through rational discourse. But what if the thrust that is behind

all human behavior is self-interest, instinctive, irrational? In that case, behavior which is ultimately beneficial both to the individual and society can be inculcated in the young through systematic training and discipline—such is the doctrine found in *Some Thoughts on Education,* published in 1693.

What Locke's final position was is difficult to say. His *Conduct of the Understanding,* on which he was at work in 1697, seems to reaffirm in large measure his confidence in the power and scope of natural human reasoning. Of his prevailing view, and with due allowance for his more extreme vacillations of opinion, we can say this. Human perversity he accepted as an ever-present fact. He dismissed, however, the theological concept of original sin. Man was not innately evil. But neither, on the other hand, was he innately good, and Locke eschewed all those theories, widespread in England by the time he died, emphasizing man's natural goodwill and benevolence. The human enterprise continued under a Divine disposition forever beyond our full comprehension. Human reason was not omnicompetent, yet its power was undoubtedly great, and by its means we were enabled to mold ourselves and our society, and gradually to enlarge our understanding of nature. Futile to ask whether of all possible worlds ours was the best or the worst. It was the one in which we found ourselves as, like Milton's Adam, we waked to consciousness, and it was the only one we were going to know this side death.

4   Locke and the Augustan Intellectual Situation[33]

Not the least interesting aspect of Locke's thought lies in the insight it affords into the intellectual situation confronting the English Augustans. The Western mind, early in our cultural history, had discovered a universe in which Reason and Nature were supreme; Reason meant the divine and eternal principle of things, a principle to which the reasoning faculty implanted in man was adjunctive; Nature stood for the universe as divinely and rationally ordered. Since the Middle Ages, however, the modern mind had been engaged in explorations—scientific, philosophic, religious—extending beyond the traditional framework, and in consequence the concept of Nature had been gradually giving ground to what can be called naturalism. Increasingly it was felt that what constituted nature was the actual events and conditions that came to be recognized in experience and through systematic observations. And nature in this sense, however little was yet known of it, lay open to sustained investigations.

By the close of the seventeenth century the work of the modern physicists, mathematicians, and astronomers, resulting in a new generally accepted view of the physical universe, seemed, along with the subsequent contribution by Newton, to be final and triumphant achievements that had laid bare within one sector the true state of nature. Meanwhile those whose dominant interest lay in man himself and in his relations with his fellow creatures and with God were becoming aware, to various degrees, that human nature might in fact be what actual human behavior showed it to be, not what a normative Nature declared it to be. Human experience—the human psyche in action—lay open, as did the physical universe, to our inquiries.

We may say that the Augustan experience—the intellectual outlook and general temper shared by the greater number of educated persons of the time—included both new concepts and old ones. There were people determined to reassert the entire system of traditional theories, and there were others who welcomed the new approaches with a sometimes revolutionary ardor, but the prevailing attitude, not necessarily arrived at in full consciousness, was one of compromise. Most accepted in great part the modern view of things and many of the theories to which such a view led, but at the same time they retained to a greater degree than they fully realized the old principles, the old certainties and values and inherited images ranging from the realm of the divine to the level of the secular.

The pact effected between science and religion, though but

a single example of the Augustan intellectual compromise, is perhaps the most striking. In no other time in modern history have the scientific and religious points of view been brought so closely into accord. The instrument by which this was frequently achieved was the argument from design, which scientists and clergy alike brandished exultantly in the faces of all whose faith seemed in danger of being undermined by the new naturalism. The universe was a natural system, yes; but how perfectly it had been constructed, how perfectly it operated! Who but God could have created it? So nature as observed phenomena was kept, and so was the Christian God.

Are we right in attributing to the Augustans as a whole, as so many have done in the past, a general attitude of shallow optimism and complacency? It is well to remember that among these Augustans there were Roman Catholics, Anglicans, and Calvinist Dissenters brought up to think of this world as a place of travail. There were also satirists who found little good among men and much evil. It is true, however, that the widespread spirit of compromise often carried with it, besides the desire to resolve conflicting views, a disposition to evade realities of a disturbing kind. It was understandable to Christian traditionalists that man was a fallen creature. But how was he to be described from a purely naturalistic standpoint? It was from such a point of view that Hobbes, the arch-materialist, had looked at him; the resulting picture was not a flattering one to man or God. There were some among the laity and the clergy who, in rejecting the conclusions to which Hobbesian naturalism led, insisted upon man's naturally benevolent nature, held to be a reflection of that love and benevolence constituting the essence of the Divine. Benevolist theories found considerable support during Locke's lifetime, especially among the Latitudinarians, and remained in evidence through the eighteenth century, though sometimes ridiculed and again sternly rejected.

What light, it can be asked, is thrown on Locke's thought when it is considered in respect of the intellectual situation of his time? Specifically, was it shaped, and if so to what extent, by the prevailing atmosphere of compromise?

We are struck by the presence in his thinking of two different systems, two different ideological matrixes, one the empirical system with sensory data its starting point, the other
the structured presuppositions and values which the traditional doctrines of the past carried with them. Locke believed
that he was approaching nature in an entirely empirical manner: ideas from sense; ideas from reflection; and out of such
ideas what is called knowledge, "the perception of the connection of and agreement, or disagreement and repugnancy of
any of our ideas."[34] We are at the mercy of what we experience through sense, reflection, and rational interpretation;
we come into the world without innate ideas, without original
sin, without original benevolence. This is radical individualism. Man is alone with his experience, his intellectual
life being the ceaseless pursuit of such understanding as the
terms of human existence allow, his moral life the application
of knowledge to his personal and social needs.

But of course man was not a naked individual, equipped
solely with the empirical mechanism. He was enfolded by
Nature. His ideas of sense flowed in upon him from a universe that existed out there beyond and in spite of all his
ignorance concerning it—a universe fashioned by God, a
purposive universe, instinct with value and descending by
graduated levels from the Divine through the angels to man.
Man lived under the eyes of God.

The accommodation of the two systems to one another was
on Locke's part effected instinctively. For him reality was, so
to speak, both systems at once. The problems involved in
bringing single out of double vision did not arise in ways that
were directly and rationally challenging. Some of the crucial
problems he sensed in his own fashion, but they came home
to him while he was tracking different game. For instance, it is
apropos of his discussion of knowledge that he sets forth the
conclusion that we have knowledge of our own existence by
intuition, of the existence of God by demonstration, and of
other things by sensation. But his demonstration of the existence of God, to which he devotes an entire chapter—Chapter
X of Book IV—comes, one feels, after the fact; it is rein-

forcement of an already deeply implanted belief in God, and simultaneously it is affirmation of the empirical condition under which we live and which permits us to proceed from sense data to reason and thus to a rationally grounded faith in God's being. In the case of the laws of morality, man's knowledge of them, and his obligation to observe them, Locke in his role of philosophic explicator did not, as we have seen, arrive at any fixed body of theory, yet his basic assumption, never shaken, was that man is forever subject, if not in one way then in some other, to the governance of God. All of Locke's varied speculations and theories about the moral situation prove to be, though contradictory, but different ways of relating natural man to God and God's Nature: man through reason recognizes his obligations imposed by Natural Law; men are everywhere seen succumbing, in disregard of all Natural Law, to the irrational forces of custom, superstition, and passion; man's basic drive, which is his ever-present desire for happiness, can induce right conduct when it functions in harmony with the understanding; since reason seldom governs in the affairs of this world, men have as their only reliance and guide the dictates of Christ and his disciples found in the Gospels.

But if this acquiescence in two substantially different perspectives clearly reflects the spirit of compromise then abroad, we could easily miss the essential Locke if we failed to perceive that anything in the nature of complacency about our beliefs, customs, and behavior, about the nature of morality, and indeed about the nature of the Divine, was foreign to him. The universe remained enigmatic; so far as we were concerned, it was an open universe, disclosing itself gradually and only partially to our rational inquiry. Though Locke paid homage to "the incomparable Mr. Newton" and other "master-builders" of the time "whose mighty designs, in advancing the sciences, will leave lasting monuments to the admiration of posterity,"[35] he found it impossible to commit himself to any master-builder's system. There was more than modesty in his description of himself as only an "under-labourer" trying to clear away "some of the rubbish that lies in

the way to knowledge": we ought all to be similarly low-flying
in our scientific and intellectual speculations. Though there
was no doubt in his mind that "the sensible parts of the
universe" offer us clear and cogent proof of God's existence,[36] and though he affirmed that "the visible marks of
extraordinary wisdom and power appear so plainly in all the
works of the creation, that a rational creature . . . cannot miss
the discovery of a Deity,"[37] he was not one of those who
pressed the argument from design nor expatiated upon the
visible beauty and order of the created world. Ours not to rest
in enjoyment, but to strive unremittingly to extend our
knowledge of the nature of things.

It must be acknowledged, however, that despite this lack of
complacency and expansive cosmic optimism, Locke suffers
today because of his air of cool detachment. He strikes us as
always the observer, the recorder, the analyst; seemingly he is
never a participant, never one caught up in the drama of
existence. We think of a modern philosopher *engagé*, like the
late Gabriel Marcel, and we lose interest in Locke. But at such
a point we have to remind ourselves that we are not to expect
from the author of the *Essay Concerning Human Understanding*
those imaginative and emotional qualities that we associate
with many of the forms of more modern consciousness. We
must come to Locke by way of the world of values and concerns which was his environment. When we do so, we find
that he was after all a deeply committed person. In his earlier
years he knew the meaning of intellectual insecurity, and
before and after his flight to Holland the meaning of personal
danger. Men were not by nature kind and benevolent; the
"state of nature" in which, according to the *Treatises of Civil
Government,* we had originally lived did not qualify as a benign
Utopia; passions and blind custom, religious prejudices and
phantasies caused by malfunction of the imagination constantly overrode reason and understanding. Yet the "candle
of the Lord," the God-given power of reason, remained with
us. "To be rational," he once wrote, "is so glorious a thing that
two-legged creatures generally content themselves with the
title."[38] There was full acknowledgment of human weakness
and of the evils springing from it, but hope was stronger than

despair. Man was always capable of reason. He could learn to live in peace with his social fellows, he could apply himself endlessly to extending his knowledge of himself and the universe in which he had been placed.

5 Locke the Writer
His Scope, the Stylistic Characteristics of His Prose, His Views on Language and Verbal Communication

The biographical sketch given in the preceding second section makes sufficiently clear the scope of Locke's writings. In the early 1660s, while still at Oxford, he had written on government and again on the law of nature. Later on, as Shaftesbury's friend and confidant, he had been called upon to draw up position papers respecting the critical issues which the country then faced. Nothing of this work had, however, appeared in print. It was during his exile in Holland that Locke the writer began, in the words of Rosalie Colie, to come out from the shadows.[39] His travels in Holland put him in touch with men of prominence in various intellectual circles, and he had the good fortune of coming to know Jean Le Clerc, the editor of *La Bibliothèque universelle*, a new periodical venture. Book reviews by Locke appeared in the new journal, as did his piece entitled "New Method of Indexing a Commonplace Book," while the eighth number contained an epitome of the *Essay Concerning Human Understanding*—the first public announcement, as it were, of his new way of ideas—which Locke had prepared and Le Clerc had obligingly translated into French. But it was only after his return to England in 1689, when he was already fifty-six, that he entered upon the great period which saw the publication of one after another of his major works—works that dealt with philosophy, religion and religious toleration, political theory, economics, and education.

The range is impressive. But with interest in linguistics and

stylistic matters so widespread today, it is the stylistic character of Locke's prose, along with his theory of language and
verbal communication, that has recently been receiving much
attention. There is, of course, some older commentary on
Locke's prose antedating the newer sort of stylistic analysis,
and such commentary sometimes strikes us as well pointed,
sometimes not. We may safely assume that most eighteenth-
century readers gave little attention to Locke's style as such,
keeping as it did at all times within the then-established
norms, but we do have the observation of Dugald Stewart,[40]
the Scottish philosopher, who remarked that the style of the
Essay was that of a cultivated man of the world, full of col-
loquial expressions which Locke "had probably caught by the
ear from those whom he considered as models of good conversation," and that this informality probably helped to bring
his philosophy to the attention of his contemporaries. In
sharp contrast is the judgment handed down in 1889 by
Edmund Gosse: Locke "as a mere writer" and setting aside
the extraordinary merits of his contributions to thought "may
be said to exhibit the prose of the Restoration in its most
humdrum form."[41] Seventy-five years later, however, Basil
Willey was finding in the style much the same features as
those seen by Dugald Stewart:[42] "[The *Essay*] is written in an
engaging tone of well-bred conversation; there are few
technicalities, and no pedantic citations of authorities. One
might call Locke the first modern English philosopher to
write like a gentleman. . . ."

Today we feel that Locke's prose is best approached in
more objective terms, which means in the first place that it is
to be considered in historical relationship with the kind of
prose style that had been emerging during the post-
Restoration period, in response to a growing demand for a
direct and unadorned manner of writing suited to the everyday needs of a new and increasingly practical-minded age. A
good many factors contributed to the rise of this plain style,
but the new interest in science stands forth conspicuously.
According to Thomas Sprat, whose then well-known *History of
the Royal Society of London* appeared in 1667, the members of

the Society were "most solicitous" regarding "their manner of discourse," taking care to avoid in their own writings "the luxury and redundance of speech" and rejecting "all the amplifications, digressions, and swellings of style" in an endeavor to deliver "so many *things,* almost in an equal number of *words.*" John Wilkins, who died Bishop of Chester, a foremost promoter of the new science and like Sprat a member of the Royal Society, put forward in his *Essay Towards a Real Character and a Philosophical Language,* published the year after Sprat's *History,* a system whereby things and words, things and linguistic signs, that is, could be perfectly related.[43] He was offering his proposal, he wrote, as a remedy against the curse of confusion and thus to facilitate mutual commerce, to improve all natural knowledge, and to spread the true knowledge of religion.

Locke's own prose is the kind of prose that had been coming into general use during his lifetime. What Gosse called the humdrum character of Restoration prose ought to be seen as resulting from a conscious effort at modernization; old-fashioned ornateness had no place; the need was for writing that conveyed one's meaning without ambiguity and with none of the unnecessary flourishes of contrived art.

Now, for those associated with the scientific movement, as Sprat and Wilkins both were, the new prose carried with it a definite theory of meaning. Sprat, as has just been pointed out, saw as the ideal way of writing one that "deliver'd so many *things,* almost in an equal number of *words.*" Language, it was assumed, was essentially a matter of individual words, each word a pointer, a symbol; effective communication was perfect accuracy of expression in the sense that the words employed pointed unmistakably at their intended targets. Language was not a matter of structure, of meanings in depth conveyed through syntax, figures of speech, and indefinable nuances. Stephen K. Land, in his recent book devoted to a study of these and related topics, has referred to the Wilkins-Sprat-Royal Society attitude as seventeenth-century linguistic atomism.[44]

Clearly, however, such atomism—if that is the right term—

was not narrowly verbal. Behind it lay a whole patterned scheme of assumptions that pictured one's statements as seeking to convey the knowledge one had gained concerning what were thought of as things having a place in the natural order of the universe.[45] In his *Philosophy of Language* (1964), W. P. Alston devotes a chapter to what he calls the "empiricist criteria of meaningfulness," his central point being that for the British empiricists a word has meaning when, and only when, an association has been established between it and an idea resulting from sense experience.

Of the empiricists mentioned by Alston, Locke is the earliest. Stephen Land, already referred to, treats Locke at length in the opening chapter of his informative book *From Signs to Propositions: The Concept of Form in Eighteenth-Century Semantic Theory*. This chapter—"The Semantics of Locke and the Royal Society"—takes up Wilkins and his *Essay Towards a Real Character and a Philosophic Language,* and proceeds to Locke's semantics as found in the third book of the *Essay Concerning Human Understanding,* a book entirely given over to the nature of words, their proper use, and their abuses. Land associates Locke with the linguistic assumptions said to characterize the Wilkins-Sprat-Royal Society tradition. Such an interpretation of Locke's position is, however, now being sharply challenged by Murray Cohen:[46] seventeenth-century linguistic theory was not wholly "atomistic," Cohen maintains; early on there was awareness that a purely intellectual factor was involved; and Locke's discussion of words and language explicitly emphasizes what the mind contributes to meaning.

However this may be, the part of the *Essay* that sounds the most familiar note today is the third book. Entitled simply "Of Words," it is in fact a treatise on meaning and communication, strikingly similar in point of view and actual substance to what is to be found in the more popular writings of many of our modern semanticists. We have been designed as sociable creatures, Locke begins by saying, and language has been given us "to be the great instrument and common tie of society." Language is articulated sound which we call words and which man uses as signs for "the ideas within his own mind" and to make these ideas known to others. Thus are human thoughts conveyed from one person to another. Though word signs can by extension be made to stand for general ideas, all words are ultimately derived from such as signify ideas resulting from sense experience. Words are used in three ways. First, to record one's own thoughts solely for the help of one's own memory. In this case it matters not what words are used, so long as there is consistency, for the sounds that are called words are "voluntary and indifferent signs" of an individual's ideas. The second use is civil—for the communication of such thoughts and ideas as may serve to uphold "the ordinary affairs and conveniences of civil life, in the societies of man." Lastly, distinctly different from the civil and requiring a much greater degree of verbal exactness, is the philosophical use, serving "to convey the precise notions of things, and to express in general propositions certain and undoubted truths, which the mind may rest upon and be satisfied with in its search after true knowledge."

In his discussion up to this point, Locke would seem, it is true, to have involved himself in some basic ambiguities. All words, we are told, "are ultimately derived from such as signify sensible Ideas." Does this mean that the words I use in my efforts to communicate with other people represent such ideas as have been established in my mind and in my mind alone? If so, in what sense am I able to communicate with others? And there is a second difficulty. Wilkins, as we have seen, sought a perfect correspondence between words and things. To this end he saw the need of a catalogue that would cover "all those things and notions to which names are to be assigned." For him, it is clear, and for the members of the Royal Society generally, the things in nature were determinate, consistent substances, making possible a common knowledge. But Locke's empiricism carried no such assumption concerning the nature of things and our "sensible Ideas."

Yet as the third book unfolds, such ambiguities as these recede. The world we live in, the world in which language is used, is a world of men interacting with one another—a civil world, a social world, the existence of which results from our ability to converse with our fellow human beings. When, however, communication is faulty, trouble arises; indeed, the greatest part of the disputes in the world are "merely verbal, and about the signification of words." At the heart of Book III lies Locke's conviction that the disputes which rend the world can be prevented through the consistent use of words, words constituting for him our language. Such a concept of language and meaning is still to be met with in the modern world; today there are those who still assume, as Locke did, that we hate and fight other men not because—as is so often and so deplorably the case—we know what they are thinking, but because we do not. Thus we find in Locke the semanticist much the same brave hope that reasonableness will prevail as in Locke the ardent advocate of toleration. But be this as it may, the world could long since have profited more than it has chosen to do from Locke's indisputably sound advice on the use of words: use no word without a clear notion of its distinct meaning; avoid the inconsistent use of a word; avoid affected obscurity and subtlety.

At this point something in the nature of an extended foot-note is not out of place. In connection with the above semantic matters the question arises of Locke's influence in the general field of literature and literary criticism in eighteenth-century England. Towards the close of his chapter on the abuse of words, Chapter X of the third book, Locke wrote as follows:

> . . . if we would speak of things as they are, we must allow that all the art of rhetoric, besides order and clearness; all the artificial and figurative application of words eloquence hath invented, are for nothing else but to insinuate wrong ideas, move the passions, and thereby mislead the judgment; and so indeed are perfect cheats: and therefore, however laudable or allowable oratory may render them in harangues and popular addresses, they are certainly, in all discourses that pretend to in-form or instruct, wholly to be avoided, and where truth and knowledge are concerned, cannot be but thought a great fault, either of the language or person that makes use of them.

For imaginative writing of any sort the implications of this statement are withering. Locke allows legitimacy only to such writing as in his words engages "truth and knowledge," and such writing has to be, in point of style, of the most severe, unadorned, and rationalistic order. Earlier in the *Essay*[47] Locke took up the by-then commonplace distinction between wit—putting ideas together with quickness and variety—and judgment—"separating carefully, one from another, ideas wherein can be found the least difference"—and voiced his suspicion of wit, which instead of reaching after truth, seeks to delight the fancy with pleasing metaphors and allusions. Wit, fancy, imaginative literature, poetry—Lockian reductionism renders them synonymous; the beauty to which they give rise is a shallow thing, lacking in truth and reason. In *Some Thoughts on Education* he expressed his low opinion of poetry in forthright terms: if a young person reveals a poetic vein, the parent "should labour to have it stifled, and suppressed, as much as may be"; Parnassus affords "a pleasant Air, but a barren Soil."

In the face of all this, Basil Willey's conclusion may seem justified. "I doubt," he has written in his *English Moralists*, "if any kind of philosophy has ever been, in all its implications, more hostile to poetry than that of Locke and his school."[48] But no kind of philosophy retains all its pristine characteristics once it enters the mainstream of thought, and Locke's did not. Locke's own severe devaluation of what we now call the artistic imagination was overlooked, and Lockian empiricism was discovered to offer an excitingly new interpretation of the role of the imagination in artistic representation of all kinds: representation, which had usually meant representation of nature—that is, of reality—tended to be seen as representation of the ideas arising out of our sense impressions. As noted in the opening section, Locke's influence on various eighteenth-century writers turned out to be considerable. Indeed, as also noted in the opening section, it is the contention of E. L. Tuveson[49] that Locke's empiricism, by endowing the mind with the power to make all its ideas out of impressions, led on to that revolutionary view of the imagination, emer-

gent in the eighteenth century and subsequently fully developed in romanticism, which rendered reality an essentially
internal experience.

One is not persuaded, however, that things happened in
precisely the way described by Tuveson, nor that Locke's
influence was in this respect so strong and so pervasive. A
more acceptable analysis of eighteenth-century critical and
aesthetic thought in relation to Locke's empiricism is given by
Stephen Land in the second chapter of his study of
eighteenth-century semantic theory. Locke's influence, he
shows, though widely reflected, does not account for many of
the strains of thought present in the more theoretical writing
of the period. The Platonic theory of imitation lived on; the
concept of the sublime drew attention; the language of passion, welcomed early in the century by the critic John Dennis
as the "very Nature and Character" of poetry, invited that
metaphorical use of language rejected so austerely by Locke.
It was Addison, in his critical papers in *The Spectator* on the
pleasures of the imagination, who really turned Lockianism
into that widely accepted aesthetic theory according to which
a multitude of pleasures, "primary" and "secondary," arise
from the real and the fanciful images in the imagination, the
real images being those caused by objects actually before us,
the fanciful ones being such as lie in the memory or are found
fictitiously.

To return, by way of conclusion, to the question of Locke's
own style, about which a little more needs to be said. His prose
can be seen, rightly enough, as exemplifying the plain style of
his era. It is likewise the prose of one who entertained a
theory of meaning and communication directly associated
with empiricism. We might in consequence expect it to ap-
proximate Sprat's idea of a style stripped to the bone, declaring so many things in almost an equal number of words.
Locke himself warned against "the art of rhetoric,"[50] acceptable insofar as it advanced order and clearness in one's discourse but otherwise only serving to insinuate wrong ideas,
move the passions, and mislead the judgment. And there are

in truth many pages of his prose—too many, most will say—
that are marked by an unrelieved plainness of style.

Yet in the face of all this Locke proves to have been something of a rhetorician in his own way, as some of the recent
studies of his style have served to emphasize. The rhetorical
nature of the writing in the *Two Treatises,* which an analysis by
Theodore Redpath reveals quite clearly,[51] has already been
mentioned. Locke's whole intent here was to advance the
liberal theory of government, and to this end he did not
hesitate to draw on the traditional rhetoric of persuasion. But
there are other kinds of rhetoric, and we may regard as
rhetorical any conscious shaping of style in order to establish
some desired relationship between writer and reader, or
speaker and auditor. Dugald Stewart, it will be recalled, drew
attention to the conversational style of the *Essay,* and
suggested that Locke's informal manner helped him to bring
his philosophy home to the general reading public; Basil
Willey has similarly spoken of the engaging conversational
tone of the *Essay.*[52] It is now possible, thanks largely to the
work of Rosalie Colie, to speak without apology of the
rhetoric of the *Essay.*

In the earliest of a series of three articles[53] it was Colie's
contention that the style of the *Essay,* so far from resembling
the style endorsed by the Royal Society, was in fact closer to
that of Montaigne; it was a social style, intentionally informal,
making for an easy relationship between Locke and his readers. In a second article, "John Locke and the Publication of
the Private," she sought to establish a Cartesian influence as
well, suggesting that in a way that was reminiscent of Descartes Locke was engaged throughout the *Essay* in building a
philosophical system on the basis of self; he wished to work
with the data of ordinary men, and accordingly chose a style
of writing that was disarmingly commonplace, a rhetoric designed, in Colie's words, "to persuade without rhetoric."

Together these two articles offer an approach to Locke as a
prose stylist that is interesting and original, though there are
some who will question the influence in this respect of Montaigne and Descartes, for which no strong evidence has really

been advanced. But the last of the three articles, "The Essayist in the *Essay*," which defines the nature of Locke's rhetoric with precision, is entirely convincing. A rhetorical attitude of humility is shown to control the first of the two prefatory epistles, while in the second epistle we find Locke playing "a delicate tonal game . . . presenting himself as a plain, stolid, slow man seriously concerned to define some steps toward truth." In the body of the *Essay* first-person pronouns, which appear repeatedly, make the writer an actor in a drama involving himself and his readers, those addressed being urged to participate in an ongoing inquiry into experiential truth. The entire work is, in fact, an "essay," a sustained effort to test, to try, through an undogmatic approach.

The *Essay Concerning Human Understanding* was once and for many years a widely read work. For understandable reasons it no longer is, yet anyone happening today to find his way into it may well discover to his surprise its thoroughly humanistic tone. It does not present itself as a discussion of things in the least remote from the common experience of ordinary people.

6   A Humanist in His Time

Among Locke's notable contemporaries there was none, one feels, more aware than he of the issues that arose during the post-Restoration decades—issues concerning public policy, as well as those of a religious and moral nature. Because he was so much a man of his time, he is not difficult to approach. His career in the world unfolded in accordance with the momentous events that took place between 1660 and the years directly following the Revolution, and is clear in its motivation and logic. His intellectual life was more complex, but in the problems he took up as a philosopher and the presuppositions present in his thought we find nothing that is in the least remote from the intellectual concerns common to the latter half of the seventeenth century.

Yet for the very reason that he is so fully associated with the contemporary historical scene and the intellectual currents of opinion that marked his period, his true genius and the unique qualities entering into it are easily lost sight of. His originality lay in a remarkable combination of factors: an unusual awareness of what was passing in the social and political world and the human values engaged, an abiding sense of man's moral and social commitments, and the ability withal to present his considered views in a way that caught and held the attention of generations of readers. The diversity of his interests and the wide range of his writings, however, make well-nigh impossible any brief summary of his achievement that is at all adequate, and Locke's present-day reputation suffers in consequence.

It is perhaps best to think of him first of all as a humanist in the broad sense—as a humanist rather than a philosophic empiricist, or a spokesman for a liberal society under limited monarchy, or an advocate of religious freedom. He was of course all of these and many other things besides, but at all times his foremost concern was with the nature of human experience. For him, experience seemed possible of occurrence only within a natural universe of which we could have only partial knowledge, yet the very fact of its occurrence affirmed the encompassing purpose—reason, power, love— of the divine.

What to us seems Locke's most serious limitation lies in his aesthetic insensibility. What we today speak of as the life of the imagination lay, seemingly, outside his comprehension. For him there was the life of moral endeavor. And there was the life of the intellect, a never-ending search for the realities lying behind our sense impressions and for the true circumstances governing man, at once a natural creature and, by virtue of his capacity for reasoning, a moral being.

Come to life today, Locke could only view with dismay the conditions that now prevail in the world community, but he would surely be assessing with amazement and delight the advances in knowledge throughout the fields of modern inquiry.

Jonathan Swift

In Defence of Order

1   Locke and Swift

There are many ways of reading Swift and reacting to him. As Sartre has recently remarked, literature is distinct from scientific communication in that it is not unambiguous, in that it carries a plurality of meanings. And it is reasonable to add that the literary writer is himself likely to present quite different appearances to different viewers. From Swift's own time to the present there has been no agreement as to the true nature of his personality or the right interpretation and evaluation of his satiric works, but throughout the years he has remained a fascinating and challenging figure. Many distinguished literary men have written about him, some in disapproval, others to establish with some objectivity his significance as Augustan satirist. In our own century we have had, for instance, T. S. Eliot's scattered but curiously interesting observations—unfortunately he never saw fit to write the critique of Swift's poetry that he once had in mind[1]—and George Orwell's ambivalent essay[2] in which Swift is first rejected as a reactionary and then admitted to the company of those writers for whose books we ought to be eternally grateful. Irish writers, naturally enough, have shown sustained interest in Swift. Shaw saw him as a kindred spirit, Joyce felt his shadowy presence, Austin Clarke paid tribute in verse and prose to Swift the poet; it has been suggested that Samuel Beckett may have been influenced in *Watt* by *A Tale of a Tub*.[3] But it is Yeats's response to Swift, profoundly imaginative, that is best remembered.

In his younger days Yeats was too much the romantic to find anything admirable in eighteenth-century literature, and by his own account he had in those days turned from Goldsmith, Burke, and Swift. What in time brought him to Swift and the other great ones of that period was a new view of eighteenth-century Ireland as a golden time of renaissance, "that one Irish century that escaped from darkness and confusion." Swift took on new meaning. Haunted by him and feeling him "always just round the next corner,"[4] Yeats read him months together. In 1929 Swift's "Epitaph" ("Swift has sailed into his rest . . .") was written, and in the following year the play *The Words Upon the Window-Pane,* in which in the course of a spiritualistic seance Swift speaks through the voice of a medium. The Introduction to *The Words Upon the Window-Pane,* a separate prose essay first published in 1931-32, is an extended discussion of Swift and a notable one. Thereafter Yeats returned time and again to Swift: in comments in the *Letters* and *Explorations,* and in unforgettable passages in the poems "Blood and the Moon" and "The Seven Sages." As Donald T. Torchiana has observed in his admirable study *W. B. Yeats and Georgian Ireland* (1966), Yeats's Swift may not be the Dean, but the pallid image that many recent scholars have been offering us is not a convincing substitute.[5]

But what bears upon the present essay most directly is not Yeats's vision of Swift in its totality but the fact that he placed Swift and Locke in direct opposition to one another. Swift, Burke, Goldsmith, and Berkeley were "four great minds that hated Whiggery" ("The Seven Sages"), whereas Locke *was* Whiggery, symbolizing as he had for William Blake that death of the spirit, that death of imagination, brought about by the triumph of empiricism in the early modern period and the resulting rise of a society recognizing only factual values. Blake hurled anathemas at Bacon, Newton, and Locke; "Descartes, Locke, and Newton," Yeats wrote, "took away the world and gave us its excrement instead."[6] In the Introduction to *The Words Upon the Window-Pane,* Swift's sinking into imbecility or madness is said to have marked the end of his and an entire epoch in the British Isles—"I can see in a sort of nightmare vision the 'primary qualities' torn from the side of Locke . . .

> Locke sank into a swoon;
> The garden died;
> God took the spinning-jenny
> Out of his side."

It is only right to point out, after due apologies to Blake and Yeats, that to see Locke as symbolic source of a bourgeois materialism spreading itself throughout eighteenth-century England is to misread Locke and the period so much of whose spirit he embodied. In his recent period study *The Augustan Vision* (1974), Pat Rogers observes that Locke has been made the prophet of eighteenth-century Whiggery "largely for accidental reasons," and that despite the traditional linking of his name and the subject of trade, he devoted little space to trade in his *Two Treatises of Government*. As we all know, Locke did make much of the rights of property, but this does not establish him as the voice of an emerging capitalist society. Rather, it shows that his concept of social order, the rule of law, and rational liberty in a society resting on the general will reflect the ideological character of that broad class of Englishmen whose forbears had, during the seventeenth century, defended their rights in confrontation with the centralized power of the executive. Even Locke's views on labor and the unemployed, set forth while he was a member of the Board of Trade, were traditional ones, not substantially different indeed from those underlying some of Swift's later tracts dealing with Ireland's social and economic ills.

Yet once this has been said in behalf of Locke, one of course hastens to acknowledge that he and Swift stood far apart from one another in most respects, two minds, two spirits separated by deep fundamental differences of temperament. Locke the philosopher and Swift the satirist held to different courses, one intellectually committed to the inquiry into the nature of human experience and the extent of one's knowledge, the other the passionate defender of established and time-honored values both secular and ecclesiastic. Locke's formulated empiricism was at odds with the traditional philosophical realism that Swift clung to, according to which our sense impressions as received in the imagination and interpreted by our rational faculty disclose the true nature of our physical world. In respect of the new science fast coming of age, Locke was a thoroughgoing modernist, and he had worked side by side with people of eminence in the fields of chemistry and medicine. Though Swift seems to have had no quarrel with Bacon[7]—Bacon's vehement rejection of scholastic pedantry and his eloquently expressed desire that the new science be directed to serving men's practical needs accorded with his own views—he had no real understanding of the scientific movement as it had developed in England since Bacon's time. Here he was an old-fashioned humanist, unshaken in his belief that our proper concern is with the moral life of man, not with the impersonal world of nature. Books celebrating the accomplishments of the men of science—of the virtuosi, as they were still often called—and depicting the modern age as one which, thanks to their efforts, was on the way to achieving superiority over all previous periods were to Swift purely and simply ridiculous, deserving of the satirist's merciless derision. Though Locke and Swift may not appear to have been so far apart in matters of stylistic simplicity and clarity of language, their similarity in this respect is really a superficial one, for Locke's anti-aestheticism, expressing itself as distrust of all writing of the imaginative order, distinguishes him radically from one like Swift, who despite his wry disparagement of poetic inspiration was himself a committed literary artist. And impossible to overlook is the irreconcilable nature of their respective views regarding religious conformity. Both were Anglicans, but whereas Locke's Latitudinarianism rendered him a foremost advocate of the widest kind of toleration, Swift thought of himself as one appointed to defend the Established Church against all dissidents, and though he accepted the fact of toleration as extended to people in England by the Act of 1689, he would yield nothing further to nonconformists, whom he steadfastly portrayed as unreasoning troublemakers, taking satisfaction in their stubborn perversities.

However, it would be inaccurate to define the relationship between Locke and Swift exclusively in terms of these radical differences. When two men so greatly endowed happen to have been contemporaries, they reveal in a number of ways the fact that they were shaped within the same matrix of cultural forces and events. If the views they held were in specific instances totally irreconcilable, such views were in the nature of reactions, however diverse, to the common circumstances of the period. But there is more than this kind of symbiotic relationship between these two Augustans. Both attacked what then went by the name of enthusiasm, both deplored the contagious irrationalism of behavior that it generated. Though Locke believed that psychological aberration of this sort could be brought under voluntary control, and frequently urged that in the interest of social harmony such irrational impulses be held in restraint through the exercise of common sense and self-discipline, yet as a physician he came to recognize that there was an order of psychic disturbance that must be accepted as lying outside all reason and beyond any rational regulation. Here Swift differed from Locke chiefly in the vehemence with which he castigated enthusiasm—for him it lay behind the intellectual, religious, and social follies of mankind—and in his unshakable conviction that men had been given the capacity to follow reason and should accordingly be held accountable for the willful refusal to do so. True madness was a different matter. He seems to have feared that he himself might go insane before he died, and his compassion for the mentally afflicted is evidenced by his bequest of a large part of his estate for the building and endowment of St. Patrick's Hospital for the insane. Yet in the eyes of the satirist, those succumbing to the follies engendered by enthusiasm behaved for all the world like madmen, and it is such that Swift has portrayed them in *A Tale of a Tub.*

Swift is so often thought of as an Augustan Tory—as in-

deed he was from 1710 onwards, having in that year fore-
sworn allegiance to the Whigs once and for all—that it is
sometimes forgotten that his political principles remained
ideologically what they had been from his early period in
Ireland—the liberal principles which had served the opponents of Charles II and James and to which Locke had given
classic expression in his *Two Treatises of Government.* Though
Swift as a traditional philosophical realist dismissed Lockian
empiricism with impatience, he recognized in Lockian political theory an enforcement of his own convictions. From the
Anglo-Irish amongst whom he had grown up, who rightly
enough saw in Toryism a threat to their own existence, he had
acquired the Whig faith, and this had been confirmed during
his subsequent years at Moor Park, Surrey, while he served as
a kind of literary secretary to Sir William Temple, an eminent, enlightened, and articulate Whig. Down to 1710, in fact,
Swift counted himself a supporter of the Whig party, though
as time passed he became increasingly uneasy over the attitude of the party leaders towards the Anglican Establishment. It was what he took to be this indifference to the needs
of the Church and their readiness, as he feared, to promote
the interests of the Dissenters at the Church's expense that
finally determined him, in the autumn of 1710, to go over to
the Tories, who had just then come into power. In doing so,
however, he had no thought of renouncing what had always
been his liberal political principles. He remained a Whig in
theory, as firmly aligned with the Locke of the *Treatises* as he
had been in 1701 when he wrote the *Discourse on the Contests
and Dissensions in Athens and Rome* in defence of the prominent
Whig leaders then under attack. Swift's Toryism was not that
of any of the pre-Revolution defenders of royal prerogative
and privilege.

Swift made only a few direct references to Locke. In these
he showed his complete accord with Locke's political writings
but a rather ambivalent attitude toward the *Essay Concerning
Human Understanding* and definite disapproval of *The Reasonableness of Christianity.* His endorsement of Locke's work on
political theory is expressed ironically in one of the famous

Drapier's Letters—the fifth, entitled *To . . . Lord Viscount Moles-worth*, which appeared late in 1724—where mention is made of Locke "and other dangerous Authors who talk of *Liberty.*" It has been pointed out, one may add, that Swift's undated *Further Thoughts on Religion* clearly parallels the first of Locke's *Two Treatises* in rejecting the standard arguments put forward by those upholding Divine Right.[8] The appearance in 1706 of a book entitled *The Rights of the Christian Church Asserted,* by Matthew Tindall, was the occasion of some caustic *Remarks* by Swift, probably written down in 1707/8, though unpublished until 1763. Tindall had at one point referred to Locke's *Essay* as a work by "a late Philosopher" which people feared would "let too much Light into the World." Swift commented that it was not the *Essay* that people disliked, but "other Workes"— an obvious reference to *The Reasonableness of Christianity;* there were people who were likely "to improve their Understanding much with *Locke*," though the *Essay* did harbor "some danger-ous Tenets, as that of [i.e., in denial of] *innate Ideas.*" Perhaps the most amusing of the *Remarks* is the one called forth by Tindall's statement that he found it necessary "to shew what is contained in the Idea of Government." This "refined Way of Speaking," wrote Swift,

> was introduced by Mr. *Locke:* After whom [Tindall] *lim-peth* as fast as he was able. All the former Philosophers in the World, from the Age of *Socrates* to ours, would have ignorantly put the Question, *Quid est Imperium?* But now it seemeth we must vary our Phrase; and since our mod-ern Improvement of Human Understanding, instead of desiring a Philosopher to describe or define a Mouse-trap, or tell me what it is; I must gravely ask, what is contained in the Idea of a Mouse-trap? . . .

Again, this time in a passage in his *Letter to a Young Gentle-man, Lately enter'd into Holy Orders* (1720), Swift took exception to matters in Locke's *Essay,* but without any facetiousness. Urging young preachers not to fill their sermons with philosophical terms and abstract, metaphysical notions, he gave it as his own experience that he had been "better enter-tained, and more informed by a Chapter in the *Pilgrim's*

Progress, than by a long Discourse upon the *Will* and *Intellect,*
and *simple* or *complex* Ideas." For Swift, common sense and
practical morality were bound up with the unsophisticated
philosophical realism from which nothing was ever to shake
him loose.

Yet these open references to Locke tell us nothing about
Locke's possible though unacknowledged influence on Swift's
own work. Some forty years ago Kenneth MacLean in his *John
Locke and English Literature of the Eighteenth Century* stated that
the influence of Locke's *Essay* is most apparent in Swift's
writings, but nothing that he advanced in support of this
contention proves very convincing. He showed, it is true, that
the writings of the Scriblerus Club, of which Swift was a
member, are often pointed by way of parody at the *Essay,* but
we have no way of knowing the nature or extent of Swift's
contributions to the joint productions with which in 1714 this
celebrated group of Tory wits was amusing itself. MacLean
threw out a few suggestions concerning possible echoes of
Locke in *Gulliver's Travels* but did not follow through on them.
More recently others have discussed at greater length the
subject of Locke and *Gulliver's Travels.* Rosalie Colie, observing in one of her interesting articles that Swift was "in his
quixotic way . . . often Lockean," drew attention to a few
places in *Gulliver's Travels* where Swift, she believed, may have
been recalling certain things in the *Essay.*[9] These resem-
blances, however, such as they are, are not very striking. But it
was not to the *Essay* that Colie looked for her chief evidence of
Locke's influence but to Locke's writings addressed to Edward
Stillingfleet, Bishop of Worcester. Stillingfleet had attributed heretical views to Locke on the basis, not of *The Reasonableness of Christianity,* but of the *Essay;* Locke had denied the
charge in a *Letter* (1697) to Stillingfleet; Stillingfleet had issued two *Answers* to Locke, and Locke in turn had published
two *Replies* (1697 and 1699). In the course of this battle of the
pamphlets Stillingfleet had attacked Locke's contention in the
Essay (III.vi passim) that the term *man* carried references not
to a real essence but only to a nominal one. In his rejoinder

Locke had written this: "I do not see how *animal rationale* can be enough really to distinguish a man from a horse." Commenting on Colie's article, Irvin Ehrenpreis agreed with her that here we have "what is probably the intellectual background of Swift's ape-man-horse seesaw."[10] It so happens, however, that we have recently become aware that the term *animal rationale*, involving comparisons between men, horses, and other animals, provided a topic that had been taken up by more than one writer of the time.[11] It seems unlikely that in the Houyhnhnm-Gulliver-Yahoo situation Swift was remembering any specific writer's treatment of the subject.

By far the most elaborate attempt to establish some sort of relationship between Locke and *Gulliver's Travels* is to be found in W. B. Carnochan's article of 1964[12] entitled "*Gulliver's Travels:* An Essay on the Human Understanding?"— Carnochan's book *Lemuel Gulliver's Mirror for Man* (1968) supplements but does not add significantly to the earlier article. Carnochan begins by advancing the theory—he calls it a suggestion—that *Gulliver's Travels* is to be seen as Swift's own *Essay Concerning Human Understanding*, an essay in which certain of Locke's concepts have been put to serious use while other aspects of Lockean theory have possibly been given satiric treatment. Lemuel Gulliver, it is said, can be taken as "a version of Lockean man." Gulliver seems to illustrate Locke's theory concerning the progress of the mind from sensation to reflection: he grows in knowledge with an "increasing aptitude for perceiving complex relationships." But Carnochan has more to say, and he begins his further discussion by posing a question: if Gulliver was indeed intended to exemplify Locke's theory of the mind, what was Swift implying thereby? It can be shown that Swift was of two opinions about Locke, readily accepting the latter's insistence on clarity of style, his dislike of mere rhetoric, and his condemnation of enthusiasm, yet on the other hand mistrustful of the Lockean new way of ideas. Swift was an epistemological realist; our knowledge is about real things and is a representation of these realities. Locke's theory leaves us with ideas but with no way of reaching behind these ideas to whatever it is that we have

ideas of; we are left confronting an epistomological dilemma.
Was it some such dilemma that Swift was perhaps implying in
the fourth voyage? Are Gulliver's experiences in the land of
the Houyhnhnms all chimeras, with no way of determining
whether as ideas they can or cannot be said to be "true"?
Carnochan leaves us with a number of suggestions eventually
resolved into questions to which he seems to feel there can be
no assured answers. There are those well versed in Swift who
will assuredly find any such conclusion entirely unsatisfac-
tory. These will protest that were there anything in *Gulliver's
Travels* intended to be commentary on Locke, commentary of
no matter what nature, we could reasonably expect it to stand
forth in unmistakable ways.

There are two other modern commentators who, like those
already mentioned, have brought to our attention what they
believe to be other possible instances of Locke's implication in
Swift's writings. R. J. Dircks, in an article entitled "Gulliver's
Tragic Rationalism,"[13] sees Gulliver's fourth voyage as an
ironic portrayal of the life of reason. Reason has here been
carried to an excess by the Houyhnhnms, who lack all imagination and are in fact pursuing a way of life that might well
have been prescribed by theorists of a Whig stamp. May it not
be that in examining their society Swift is reflecting on the
social and political philosophy of Locke, foremost of Whig
theorists, whose speculations are as devoid of human feeling
and emotions as the principles professed by the reasoning
horses? The possibility that Dircks raises is interesting chiefly
because of its novelty in suggesting the presence in *Gulliver's
Travels* of a definitely anti-Lockean element. But the underlying assumption here is that the rational values declared by the
Houyhnhnms are not meant to be taken seriously, and such
an assumption is not one that finds anything like universal
acceptance among present-day students of Swift.

More to the point is W. A. Speck's suggestion in his *Swift,* a
short critical study appearing in 1970, that there are passages
in *A Tale of a Tub* which parody Locke. Though it seems
unlikely (contrary to Speck's belief) that Section IX of the
Tale, the great "Digression Concerning . . . Madness," was

written with Locke in mind,[14] it may well be that the "Epistole
Dedicatory" of the *Tale* is in part a parody of the "Epistle to
the Reader" which Locke prefixed to his *Essay*.

But as we review all that has been advanced by those who
would show that Swift's work gives evidence of Locke's influence, we are not greatly impressed. Swift had read Locke and
was quite aware of his commanding presence in the Augustan
intellectual scene. Some of Locke, the political theory, he
accepted without demur, whereas in the *Essay* he found a
mistaken epistemology, and in *The Reasonableness of Christianity*, in all probability, dangerously unsettling views. But he
seems to have left Locke alone. It is not clear that he ever
borrowed from him significantly, and he certainly never
made him an unmistakable object of his satire.

Apropos of the relationship of Swift and Locke, one
further observation is in order. Both of them, regardless of
whatever similarities and differences are discernable, were
men who were fully alive to the interests and urgencies, political and intellectual, of their time. Locke, as has been
suggested in the preceding study devoted to him, may be
thought of as an Augustan humanist in a broad sense, seeking
to understand how knowledge is acquired, what the springs of
human conduct are, and the nature of our social respon-
sibilities and our obligations to Divine precepts. Furthermore,
he took an active part in the events leading up to the Revolution, and thereafter served dutifully in a public post. His
passionate interest in things outside him, in the intellectual
and moral-ethical problems uppermost in the minds of his
contemporaries, was characteristic of the greater Augustans.

It is true that Locke's liberalism seems to differentiate him
from Swift, one of the great voices of Augustan conservatism,
and it is for such conservatism—essentially ethical, lacking in
sympathy for the new scientific inquiries, its view of human
nature deeply colored by Christian pessimism, and looking to
traditional ways and values for guidance—that some present-day scholar-critics would reserve the term *Augustan hu-
manism*. Yet despite their widely different conceptions of the

human situation, Locke and Swift both sought to influence public attitudes and to affect the courses of contemporary affairs. Yeats, looking back upon the *fin de siècle* group of writers he had been associated with in London, came to think of them as "the tragic generation"—unstable, overwrought people, insistent upon emotion unrelated to any public interest.[15] Neither Locke nor Swift was self-enclosed in this fashion. Both made themselves a part of the life about them.

2   Swift's Life
Facts and Speculations

Swift's career as a writer and as a public figure in England and Ireland falls into a few distinctly marked periods. Born in Dublin in 1667 of English parentage, he was a posthumous child, dependent throughout his youth on the generousity of his paternal uncles. He attended Kilkenny School, then the nearest thing in Ireland to an aristocratic English public school, and Trinity College, Dublin, where he took the B.A. in 1686. As a candidate for an advanced degree, he was still in residence at Trinity College when the widespread disorders that were spreading through Ireland in the wake of the Revolution of 1688 caused him, along with many of the Anglo-Irish, to seek safety in England. It was at Moor Park, Surrey, that he shortly found employment as a kind of literary secretary to the retired diplomat Sir William Temple.

The ensuing ten years were all-important ones in Swift's development. Though his association with Temple extended down to the latter's death early in 1699, he found reason on two separate occasions to return to Ireland, and it was there that he took orders in the Anglican Church and, early in 1695, was ordained priest. His earlier years at Moor Park saw him struggling manfully to become a poet. The verse he then wrote—odes in the manner of Cowley, together with some more regular pieces—is of some interest biographically and does contain passages of genuine power, but its shortcomings were only too evident, and in disgust he took leave of the Muse. It was during his latter years with Temple that he found his true talent, as he turned from verse to prose satire. *A Tale of a Tub,* second only to *Gulliver's Travels* as a satiric achievement, had been virtually completed by the time of Temple's death in January 1699, though it did not receive publication until 1704. When it appeared, anonymously, it created something of a stir; there were those like Addison who discerned not only its wit and its extraordinary original- ity but also its underlying seriousness of purpose; others, thrown off by its unconventialities of form and treatment, indignantly pronounced it an unforgivably scandalous book.

The *Tale* is a tripartite work, comprising the *Tale* proper, *The Battle of the Books,* and *A Discourse Concerning the Mechanical Operation of the Spirit.* The *Battle,* a mock-heroic account of a literary squabble, casts ridicule upon two writers, William Wotton and Richard Bentley, who had recently faulted one of Temple's essays. Temple and his supporters are represented as defenders of the right and universal standards in taste and literature first defined by the ancients; Wotton and Bentley and those of their party appear as ill-mannerd upstarts blind to all but modern culture and its innovative ways. *The Dis- course* has as its satiric target the religious enthusiasts of the period and their preaching and manner of worship. The longest and most brilliant of the three satiric pieces is the *Tale* itself, much of it a parody of modern writing and concerned throughout and in its own amazing way with what Swift was later to refer to as "the numerous and gross corruptions in Religion and Learning." In form, the work is a labyrinth of prefaces, dedications, introductions, together with the story of the three brothers, Peter, Martin, and Jack, a story broken up into Sections between which are sandwiched a series of so-called Digressions. The actions—or better, the antics—of Peter and Jack are meant to exemplify the errors and excesses which Anglicans of this time traditionally attributed to Roman Catholicism on the one hand and the Dissenters, followers of John Calvin, on the other, while Martin embodies that *via*

media between the two extremes—a rational moderation—
which, it was said, the Church of England stood for. The
disorders of learning are taken up in the Digressions, which
deal with absurdities on the part of modern writers, critics
(Wotton and Bentley turn up again) and all those who
through mistaken zeal, inducing a quasi-madness, have lost
touch with reality.

Temple's death brought the Moor Park period to a close.
Before long Swift was back in Ireland, receiving early in 1700
several appointments in the Irish Church, the most important
of which was to the vicarage of Laracor, not far from Dublin.
Though he showed due concern for his duties and respon-
sibilities as Vicar of Laracor, in the course of the ensuing ten
years he was frequently away in England, sometimes for extended periods, leaving a curate in charge. His visits to London, some of them at the behest of the Irish Bishops, who
were seeking certain favors for the English government, kept
Swift abreast of public affairs and marked his emergence as a
pamphleteer. *A Discourse of the Contests and Dissensions in Athens
and Rome,* which was published in 1701, though without the
author's name, was at once a defense of the Whig lords then
being threatened with impeachment by a Tory House of
Commons and a statement of liberal political principles of the
sort historically associated with the Whigs. In 1709 came a
reforming tract, the *Project for the Advancement of Religion, and
the Reformation of Manner.* The forthright *Sentiments of a
Church-of-England Man* and the satiric *Argument against Abolish-
ing Christianity* were withheld until 1711, appearing then in a
volume of his miscellaneous verse and prose.

Swift was in London throughout 1708, by which time he
had acquired something of a name as a writer of talent and a
wit, and the Bickerstaff pamphlets that were now appearing,
directed with humour and lethal effectiveness against the
popular astrologer John Partridge, added to his reputation.
He had also been writing verse again, but no longer in the
high manner. His new subjects were such as lent themselves to
witty and informal treatment. "The Humble Petition of Fran-
ces Harris" (1701), the two versions of "Baucis and Phile-

mon" (the earlier one, probably composed in 1706, never appeared in Swift's lifetime; the latter appeared in 1709 in Steele's *Tatler,* No. 9) are all memorable examples of the kind of minor poetry the Augustans excelled at. When Swift left London in the spring of 1709 to return once more to Ireland, he had achieved a recognized place in Addison's circle of Whig writers and had just helped Steele, with whom he was at this time on the friendliest terms, in getting the *Tatler* under way.

The months that followed were trying ones. His efforts while in England to advance the interests of the Irish Church had come to nothing. The cold indifference he had encountered on the part of the Whig administration had left him embittered as well as apprehensive—apprehensive that the Whigs then in power were ready to give greater consideration to the Dissenters than to the Established Church.

It was in this mood that he again found himself in London at the beginning of September 1710, at the moment when the political scene was undergoing a dramatic change. The Whigs, long in power, had fallen from favor, and a Tory ministry, headed by Robert Harley (later Earl of Oxford) and Henry St. John (later Viscount Bolingbroke) was taking over, resolved to bring the long-drawn-out war with France, the War of the Spanish Succession, to a conclusion. Harley, in need of someone able to publicize effectively the steps being taken by the ministry, approached Swift, and through the simple expedient of promising aid to the Church of Ireland won over to the Tory side a writer who proved to be one of the greatest of all political journalists.

One of Swift's first publications after this reappearance of his in London was not, however, political at all. "A Description of a City Shower," a verse piece admirably complementing his earlier "Description of the Morning," appeared in the *Tatler* in mid-October before the spirit of party had as yet driven Steele and Swift apart. Early in November, however, Swift was entrusted with the editorship of the Tory weekly, *The Examiner,* a post which he held into June 1711, writing in all thirty-two numbers of the journal. His purpose in these articles was to drive home the necessity of a peace treaty with France, and to this end he attached with great effectiveness and little scruple all those—including, notably, the Duke of Marlborough—who were for continuing the war at whatever cost. Swift brought to a close his journalistic campaign for peace with his famous *Conduct of the Allies,* which appeared in December 1711 just before Parliament voted to accept the peace proposals submitted by the ministers.

After this ministerial triumph as before, a steady flow of verse, squibs, and minor pamphlets, all political, all polemical, came from Swift's pen. Having served the ministry well, Swift now awaited the reward, which came at last in April 1713 with his appointment as Dean of St. Patrick's Cathedral in Dublin. The post was a substantial one, but Swift had hoped for something different—a bishopric, possibly, or an incumbency in England. The Queen, however, had blocked other preferment—St. Patrick's she did not control—out of resentment occasioned, as we now know,[16] by Swift's ruthless attack on the Duchess of Somerset in his poem "The Windsor Prophecy."

The Tory ministers were by this time at odds with one another. Swift, whose installation as Dean had not kept him long in Dublin, strove fruitlessly to restore harmony among his friends, but in the end gave up and retired to the country. Queen Anne's death on 1 August 1714 left the Tory party in ruins and made way for the triumphant Whigs, who were to hold sway throughout the rest of Swift's life.

What may be regarded as the final period in Swift's life extended from 1714, when he took up residence at his deanery, adjacent to St. Patrick's Cathedral, down to his death on 19 October 1745. Save for two brief visits to England in 1726 and 1727 he remained in Ireland throughout these years, an exile, as he liked to believe. Yet despite his disappointed hopes and the unpropitious circumstances of much of his life in Dublin, he did not succumb to futile bitterness and lethargy. Once restored to his full energies, he turned again to public affairs, and in consequence of his pamphlets and public letters established himself as Ireland's Patriot Dean. He was no less active as a literary writer: *Gulliver's Travels* and *A Modest Proposal* both fall within the period, as do a number of other prose works, satirical and otherwise, together with a surprisingly large body of verse that includes, along with much of a trivial nature, some of his most impressive poems.

Whether Swift's title "Irish Patriot" is deserved or not is still being debated. It is true that he spoke as a member of a highly privileged, all-powerful minority, otherwise known as the English Garrison in Ireland—English, not Irish, in blood and cultural inheritance; Protestants, not Roman Catholics, in religion; but Protestants of the Established Church, not Protestant dissenters. Regardless of all this, the Irish people as a whole have in the past accepted him as one of their own, and for at least two manifest reasons. Swift, though not the first one in or out of Ireland to call in question the assumption underlying England's colonial politics, laid down an unforgettable challenge when in the *Drapier's Letters* he invoked the natural right of a country to freedom under its own parliament. And along with this political liberalism went a trenchant sense of social and economic realities too willingly disregarded by the Irish themselves.

The first of his many Irish pamphlets of this period was *A Proposal for the Universal Use of Irish Manufacture,* which appeared in 1720. Four years later came the famous series of *Drapier's Letters.* The occasion of these was a grant which had recently been issued by the authorities in England to William Wood, empowering him to issue a new supply of copper coins for use in Ireland. The Irish protested vehemently, maintaining that the introduction of the new coins would have disastrous consequences. In the *Drapier's Letters* Swift touched on all the aspects of this affair as seen by the opponents of the grant. Long practiced in the art of political rhetoric, he dwelt on what were said to be the follies of the scheme, on its dangers, on its absurd features; he reviled Wood; he called on his readers to refuse the coins if issued; and in the climactic fourth *Letter* (22 October 1724), while affirming loyalty to the English sovereign, he denied Ireland's dependency on the English parliament. As for Wood's halfpence, the remedy lay in the hands of the Irish themselves: ". . . by the Laws of God, of NATURE, of NATIONS, and of your own Country, you ARE and OUGHT to be as FREE a People as your Brethren in *England.*"

The entire list of Swift's Irish writings is a long one, testifying to a concern on his part that remained undiminished through his active years. Many of the items are straightforward in approach, intended to bring to public attention existing social and economic conditions or to put forward practical recommendations. But of the shorter pieces the one that has with reason outlasted all the others is his masterpiece of ironic protest, *A Modest Proposal* (1729).

However, Swift's interests during the 1720s and '30s were by no means confined to Irish affairs. In his *Letters to a Young Gentleman, Lately enter'd into Holy Orders* (1720) he touched, often with wry humour, on topics of concern to every clergyman going about his usual duties, and in *A Letter to a Young Lady, on her Marriage* (1723) he undertook to give advice on matrimonial and domestic matters. *The Letter to a Young Poet* (1721) is distinguished from the others by its broad and sustained irony, and though Swift's authorship has in our day been questioned, it is hard to believe that anyone else then writing could have imitated a Swiftian style so closely. At what precise time *Gulliver's Travels* was actually begun we do not know—perhaps during those months in 1713-14 when the Scriblerus Club was meeting—but his correspondence shows that in any event he was at work on it in 1721. In August 1725 he announced that the *Travels* was finished, and he carried the completed manuscript with him when he once again visited England in 1726. That summer he saw much of his old friends and visited Pope at the latter's residence at Twickenham. He departed for home in mid-August. The manuscript was delivered to the publisher by Pope and others, and the first edition of *Gullver's Travels*, in two octavo volumes, appeared on 28 October 1726. Its immediate success was reported to Swift, now in Dublin, by the friends of his who had assisted in its publication.

But Swift's achievement as a writer during the decades

following his return to Ireland as Dean of St. Patricks's must be seen as including a truly extraordinary body of verse—extraordinary by reason of volume, scope, arresting differences in treatment, and most of all because of the impressive character of so many of the compositions. The antiromantic theme, ruthlessly developed in such earlier poems of the period as "Phyllis, Or, the Progress of Love" and "The Progress of Beauty" (both 1719), he returned to time and again, notably in the still-controversial "Stephen and Chloe," "A Beautiful Young Nymph Going to Bed," and "Cassinus and Peter" (all 1731). There are many playful or witty trifles, written about or for his friends and acquaintances. There is a good deal of clamourous verse associated with the Wood affair and later Irish episodes. Swift had never been lacking in a sense of self, but the course his life had taken since the beginning of his "exile" in 1714 inclined him more strongly than ever towards self-commentary. A number of the poems have as their chief subject the Dean himself, the best known being the "Verses on the Death of Dr. Swift" (1731), recently the subject of much analytical criticism. The composite portrait that results from all these pieces is of one conscious of his preeminent stature both as a public figure and as a literary artist but aware always of the ironies conspiring to reduce one's self-esteem.

Of the years immediately preceding Swift's death on 19 October 1745 there is little to record. He remained active well into the 1730s, and as he entered upon his seventieth year in the autumn of 1736 a celebration was held in Dublin to mark the event. Though he had for years suffered from the affliction known as Ménière's disease, involving a disorder of the semicircular canals of the ears and producing periods of giddiness, nausea, and deafness, his final incapacitation appears to have been the result of the usual physical deterioration accompanying old age and of, finally, a paralytic stroke. In August 1742 he was found of unsound mind and incapable of caring for himself, though he lived on for three more years, dying on 19 October 1745. He was buried in St. Patrick's Cathedral with the epitaph which he himself had written—his ultimate act of self-dramatization—affixed to the nearby wall.

Since the foregoing account has been confined, by intention, to objective facts attaching to Swift's career as a writer and public figure, a brief supplement is in order concerning certain episodes in his private life the exact nature of which remains in doubt and which have, for this reason, given rise to a body of sensational speculation.

Esther Johnson, or Stella as Swift later called her, the daughter of Temple's widowed housekeeper, was a girl of eight when Swift first came to Moor Park. According to a later statement of his he "had some hand in her education, by directing what she should read, and perpetually instructing her in the principles of honour and virtue." Shortly after Temple's death she and Rebecca Dingley, likewise of the Moor Park entourage, moved to Ireland and took up residence together in Dublin. From then on, until her death in 1728, she and Swift were constantly in touch with one another, meeting socially when Swift was in Ireland, addressing verses to one another, corresponding when he was away—the *Journal to Stella* consists of Swift's letters to her and Rebecca Dingley sent from London during the exciting months following his return to England in September 1710. It was during his 1707-9 sojourn in London that Vanessa, otherwise Esther Vanhomrigh, a girl of Dutch descent born in Dublin, appeared in his life. On her side at least, what began in friendship turned into passion, and the consequent change in the relationship between the two became the subject of Swift's poem *Cadmus and Vanessa* (1713), which, though it allows of different interpretations, may reasonably be taken to mean that for Swift there was to be only friendship. Later on and in spite of his admonitions, Vanessa followed him to Ireland, the letters which she thereafter wrote him revealing her uncontrollable passion, though before she died—in June 1723—she had apparently turned against him, since there is no mention of him in her will.

These are the bare facts. What has been made of them is

something else again. According to an early rumor, Swift and Stella were secretly married in 1716, the marriage remaining, however, one in name only. How was such a strange affair to be accounted for? Stella, it was sometimes asserted, was Temple's illegitimate daughter, and because of this Swift could not bring himself openly to acknowledge the marriage. Another interpretation involved Vanessa, whose association with Swift was so resented by Stella, it was said, that the latter demanded such recognition as a nominal marriage conferred. There were those who held that the relationship between Swift and Vanessa was, or had at one time been, a physical one; it was even affirmed that they had had a child, who ended up in the care of the compassionate Stella. But the most lurid of the theories that have found a place in this cycle are two concerning the blood relationship of Swift and Stella. This version declared Sir William Temple to be the father of both of them by different mothers, a fact of which Swift and Stella were totally ignorant until the truth was obligingly disclosed to them moments after they had been united in marriage. In another and more recent version Swift and Stella are found to be not half-brother and half-sister but half-uncle and half-niece, Stella remaining Temple's illegitimate daughter but Swift becoming the illegitimate son not of Temple but of Temple's father![17]

All of these rumors and theories revolve around an assumed marriage between Swift and Stella, and all of them are rightfully suspect in that hearsay evidence and only hearsay evidence is brought forward. However, a somewhat different line of speculation and one more deserving of serious attention should be mentioned. Here the problem is not that of a marriage—there may or may not have been one—but of Swift's celibacy in the sense of sexual abstinence. How is this to be explained? In his Introduction to *The Words Upon the Window-Pane* Yeats considered the question and reviewed the different answers that have been proposed from time to time. Scott suggested a physical defect, an explanation which seemed to Yeats, for reasons not given, an "incredible" one; Lecky thought the cause may have lain in Swift's dread of madness; someone else believed that Swift had contracted syphilis not long after 1699; Shane Leslie did not consider Swift's relation to Vanessa platonic and thus rejected the notion of sexual self-denial. (Others, not here referred to by Yeats, have held that Swift was a homosexual.) As for Yeats, he could find (so he wrote in this Introduction to his play about Swift) no satisfactory solution: "Swift, though he lived in great publicity, and wrote and received many letters, hid two things which constituted perhaps all that he had of private life: his loves and his religious beliefs." Yet Yeats did, after all, form his own imaginative interpretation, for in the play itself Swift rejects love of flesh with Vanessa for love of mind with Stella.

3   Swift Under Analysis
Some Modern Pronouncements

The intent of the present essay is to view Swift as an Augustan among other Augustans, standing on common ground, vehemently rejecting many contemporary moods and trends, defending just as vehemently certain inherited values, concerned at once with the problems of his own time and a timeless, human condition. Such an approach asks that we direct our attention at the public rather than the private Swift—at what he did as a man of action, at his stated views and convictions, and at his writings regarded as literary achievements to be considered in and for themselves.

There are many, however, who regard such an approach as coldly academic and incapable of achieving anything in the nature of imaginative insight. Frequently Swift commentators and critics have shown less desire to assess his achievements in objective terms than to explore his personality as they see it revealing itself in the events of his life and finding expression through his writings. The romantic Swift, a fascinating, exciting, sometimes enigmatic, often repellent figure, emerged long ago. It was such a figure that Thackeray set before the nineteenth-century reading public in his well-known essay. It

is true that Swift scholarship has worked, whether intentionally or not, against the romantic myth, and much modern
criticism has been emphasizing the formalistic, not the subjective, aspects of Swift's writings. Yet the romantic Swift has
lived on, presenting an irresistible subject for the kind of
internal exploration that popular Freudianism has encouraged. The various interpretations of Swift's psychological
make-up that have been advanced in recent years show many
differences among themselves, yet in spite of this they have
worked together to push into the foreground the factors of
personality rather than any nonsubjective aspects. In consequence, one theory or another concerning the Swiftian
psyche will be found to underlie many of the modern discussions of the Dean.

Theorizing of this nature, it turns out, has frequently been
directed primarily at Swift as a person, with only broad reference to his literary works, while at other times more at the
person disclosed in and unconsciously conditioning specific
writings. W. A. Speck, whose study of Swift appeared in 1970,
is one who has taken the first approach. "It is as misleading,"
he tells us, "to say that Swift was normal as it is to call him
mad"; the fact remains, however, that "he was a deeply disturbed man." Similar, up to a point, is the position taken by T.
G. Wilson in an essay on "Swift's Personality" (1962)[18]: although Swift was not insane, he was undoubtedly a
psychopath. Wilson then turns to the writings to confirm this
morbidity and cites "the constant references to the bodily
excreta" as evidence of "a pathological obsession"; Swift was
an obsessional, and such was the form his obsession took. In
his *Jonathan Swift* (1973), David Ward has discerned Swift's
disorder to be autoeroticism, and has suggested a transfer-
ence of his guilt feeling into his satiric attack on Inspiration.
T. G. Wilson, in the article referred to above, reminds us that
some have believed that Swift was a homosexual, a suggestion
that Wilson himself rejects on the ground of Swift's involvement with women.

The scatology present both in Swift's verse and prose has
occasioned endless discussion and has frequently resulted in

psychoanalytic theorizing based on what are taken to be the unconscious self-revelations present in his writings. T. G. Wilson, as we have just seen, regards Swift's references to bodily excretions as manifestation of a pathological obsession, and a similar interpretation has so often been placed on these details that it can be said to represent the commonly accepted view. At this point it should be noted, however, that those who in recent years have written on the subject of Swift's scatology have by no means all agreed that it arose from any particularly pathological condition. To Yeats, it pointed to the cultural dryness into which Swift had the misfortune to be born: his absorption in the useful—Yeats refers to *The Tale of a Tub,* having in mind presumably the insistence there upon the rational and the practical—compelled Swift's nature to become coarse: "The man who ignores the poetry of sex, let us say, finds the bare facts written up on the walls of a privy, or himself is compelled to write them there. But all this seems to me of his time, his mere inheritance."[19] Scatological satire, including Swift's, is the subject of an entire study by J. N. Lee (1971). One of Lee's conclusions is that the scatological elements in Swift's poems, when seen in relation to similar elements in Dante and in Rabelais, show Swift to be "as moral and as humanistic as either of his illustrious predecessors." Norman O. Brown, in his well-known *Life Against Death* (1959), finds in Swift's scatology "startling anticipation of Freudian theories about anality, about sublimation, and about the universal neurosis of mankind." Swift, in effect, was an eighteenth-century Freudian sociologist, "the excremental vision of the Yahoo" being "substantially identical with the psychoanalytic doctrine of the extensive role of anal eroticism in the formation of human culture." In one of the most recent essays on this subject, "The Comedy of Swift's Scatological Poems" by T. B. Gilmore, Jr.,[20] the mock-heroic allusions running throughout Swift's scatological poems are said to suggest that tolerance and playfulness inherent in the comic outlook.

The psychoanalytical approach to Swift through specific works of his has, however, taken in much more than the scatological poems, and has proceeded hand in hand with the kind of close textual analysis that modern criticism has pro-

moted. More than anyone else, F. R. Leavis has led the way
here. In "The Irony of Swift," an article of lasting importance
which first appeared in 1934,[21] Leavis submitted to detailed
examination certain parts of *A Tale of a Tub,* and concluded
from his reading of the passage in the "Digression on Madness" concerning the peaceful state "of being a Fool among
Knaves" that the explosive power of the irony at work here is
wholly negative, leaving nothing positive behind. It would, of
course, be quite incorrect to associate Leavis with psychoanalytic criticism. The negation revealed in *A Tale of a Tub* is,
however, the negation of one who denied life, and in the wake
of Leavis, critic after critic has been encouraged to find at
various points in the Swift text indications of psychological
disturbance or definite abnormalities. Though Leo Spitzer
has no place among Swift critics, his use of stylistic analysis to
uncover a writer's psychic pattern—he found that Henri Bar-
busse betrayed himself through his metaphorical expression
as an erotic type—may well have been another contributing
factor. Erik Erikson's so-called psycho-historical approach can
also be cited, though his 1958 study of Luther is an example
of psychological theory (here the theory of identity crisis)
applied in the broadest way and not through textual analysis.
C. J. Laing's inquiries into schizophrenic and other varieties
of human experience, and what he has had to say about
society as an organization of repression, are likewise present
in the background influencing recent Swift criticism.

But the critics who perhaps most clearly illustrate the
psychoanalytic approach entailing direct reference to specific
passages are John Traugott and C. J. Rawson, both of whom
have contributed highly stimulating essays appearing in
Focus: Swift (1971, a collection of recent critical discussions
edited by Rawson). Traugott's essay "A Tale of a Tub," an
analysis of Swift based on the *Tale,* is a most provocative
critique, unyielding in its psychoanalytic dogmatism and carried through with great verve. Academic critics of the past
few decades are taken severely to task for having viewed Swift
so largely in terms of his cultural background and the tradition of satiric art while playing down his personality. Thackeray, for all his faults, succeeded as the academics do not in

perceiving with clarity the paradoxial qualities of Swift the man. What Traugott finds at the center of Swift's personality is a "strange mixture" of institutional piety and a fundamentally subversive and pyrrhonistic imagination. The evidence lies in *A Tale of a Tub* and the psychic forces entering into the composition of this early satire, described as "a *tour de force* of black humour" that leaves us with anxiety as the final reality. The anxiety thus communicated has been generated by the ambiguities inherent in the *Tale* and reaching back to the author himself: there is satiric repudiation, carrying with it established, institutional values; simultaneously there is imaginative scepticism that undercuts accepted proprieties.

In his essay entitled "Swift, Our Contemporary," also given in *Focus: Swift,* Traugott refers with admiration to Erik Erikson and his study of the young Martin Luther, and expresses the conviction that a theory of history founded on psychoanalysis, "the latest and most productive modern turn of criticism," is "wholly pertinent to an explication of Swift." Not surprisingly, the explication that Traugott gives in his essay on the *Tale* follows the lines set by Erikson. The youth who found his way to the Temple establishment at Moor Park was one who had known no real affection, who acknowledged no ties to anyone or anything; he was a kind of "psychological bastard." The association with Temple had its effect. Finding in Temple what he had not found before, he mimicked his patron; he made Temple's views his own; he outsnobbed the aristocratic writer whom he served and became like him scornful of the search for knowledge.

As Traugott proceeds with his analysis, he endeavors to show how all three pieces in *A Tale of a Tub*—the *Tale* proper, *The Battle of the Books,* and *The Mechanical Operation of the Spirit*—reveal the ambivalence and anxiety that Swift's experiences induced. As satirist and ironist Swift made himself one of the elect—he, an arriviste—writing for gentlemen and heaping scorn on modern letters, modern scholarship, and modern science. The high moral purpose into which his hatred of the vulgar had been sublimated was genuine enough; there was nothing of conscious hypocrisy about

Swift's defense of traditional culture. Yet he was in deep conflict with himself, self-hating despite the attitude of superiority he had assumed in his role of satirist, in sympathy, beneath the surface, with all the radical individualism and irrational energies displayed by the enemy; the parodist, the satirist "begins to think in the pattern of his victims whose radical notions of life and personality become his own." So the psychological bastard, the deprived young Irishman, triumphs; his nihilism declares itself, shattering all polite illusions of sanity and order.

C. J. Rawson has written extensively on Swift, and his commentary, to be found in a number of separate essays—two are included in *Focus: Swift*—constitute the most exciting Swift criticism to have appeared in recent years.[22] Even those who reject the psychoanalytic approach that he has used and who are forced to take exception to his central conclusions must nevertheless acknowledge the force and brilliance of his writing. Though the Swift that he gives us never ceases to be an eighteenth-century figure, to be seen in association with Fielding and Johnson, he has simultaneously been brought into our own time and rendered subject to the kinds of emotional experiences recognized by André Breton as black humor, or found in a fictional character like Kurtz in Conrad's *The Heart of Darkness,* or analysed by R. D. Laing in one or another of his studies of the psychologically disturbed.

A few major themes run through Rawson's analysis. One has to do with insanity—both the madness exhibited by the whole world and the condition of madness as evinced in the individual. Another lies in the implication that social order, institutional stability, and the determination to protect and preserve them are all, from a psychological point of view, evidence of a rigid authoritarianism, frequently ruthless— sadistic, even—in its enforcements. Still another is that of self-involvement on Swift's part in those disorders and radical irrationalities that are being rejected in scorn and ridicule— an involvement working beneath the surface, accompanied by guilt feeling and an agonizing questioning of order itself. Swift and Johnson both at times felt menaced by insanity;

both "were quick to feel that their view of a universal 'madness' implicated themselves also."[23] Swift's *Some Thoughts on
Free-thinking,* as Rawson reads it, is a self-implicating generali-
zation signalling unconsciously the writer's own doubt, a
doubt psychologically determined and radically incurable.[24]
Swift and Johnson are again found alike in that the moral
view that was theirs rested on authoritarian solidity, while for
both of them doubt was to be subdued by discipline or at least
concealed.[25] Swift's treatment of the enemy betrays a kinship
therewith that he has not brought himself to acknowledge; his
"castigating attitudes" and postures are those which "in some
ways and with varying degrees he himself mirrors elsewhere."
Though he preached moderation and advanced the middle
way in society, law, and the State religion, he did so with a
passionate extremism that bespoke a deep wish for the ex-
termination, now of the entire race of troublemakers, "now of
selected types."[26]

Rawson makes much of what he calls Swift's capacity for
indulging in "certain extravagant cruelties of imagination"
which he allows to go beyond the realm of his satire and
indeed beyond morality.[27] By way of illustration Rawson
points to the flayed woman in the ninth section, the "Digression on Madness," of *A Tale of a Tub.*[28] In this passage the
speaker—a character, be it noted, in the satiric scene that is at
this point being enacted—has just declared the outside of
things to be preferable to the inside, the truth of which, he
declares, "I have been . . . convinced from some late experiments. Last week I saw a woman flayed, and you will hardly
believe how much it altered her person for the worse." Here,
we are told, the flayed woman does not merely serve the
argument but spills over it into a domain of cruel fantasy.
There is "a haze of *extra* hostility" betokening a distinct
animus against the victim. Swift's "gratuitous shocks" are, in
fact, to be associated with the literature of cruelty.

Such an analysis of Swift, conducted in distinctively modern
terms, places him pathologically in a modern context. Yet, as
has already been pointed out, Rawson has not been oblivious
of the eighteenth-century background. The so-called "gloom

of the Tory satirists" touched not only Tories and satirists but many of the most representative Augustan writers, who despite the easy confidence with which they sometimes took their refined age for granted, sensed that the enemy, an inhumanity threatening to everything making for civilization, was found everywhere, and not only around them but within themselves. And Rawson pays tribute to Swift as "perhaps the only great writer of the century whose style is fairly consistently charged . . . with a note of anguished yet passionately committed loyalty to the cherished values under threat."[29] And the threat lay as much in himself as in others. We might well, it is suggested, "entertain the thought that Swift . . . was and sensed that he was, in all rebellious recalcitrance himself Yahoo."[30]

It will be seen from the foregoing review that the modern analysis of Swift reflects no generally agreed-upon theory of psychology. Though the critics who have been applying what can loosely be called literary psychoanalysis show in various degrees the general influence of Freud, they are scarcely to be described as thoroughgoing Freudians. They are amateur psychologists, and they differ from one another both in their ways of approach and in their findings. They are at one, however, in accepting and giving renewed support to the romantic view of Swift which sees him as a person who exhibits in his life and in his writing deep emotional disturbances of one sort or another.

There are those, however, who refuse to accede to the romantic interpretation in any of its many versions—an interpretation which they insist gives a distorted view of Swift's personality and of his achievement in and outside the realm of letters. This refusal does not necessarily signify a deep-seated aversion to everything falling under the head of literary psychoanalysis. The insights which Swift's critics of the psychoanalytic school profess to have gained—insights into his inner life and the subjective import of certain of his writings—may in some instances be valid ones and in any case deserve consideration. But the emphasis here has rested on Swift's private neuroses to an undue degree, and in disregard of those other and greatly significant kinds of neuroses now broadly referred to as discontents of civilization.

We have come to recognize that all of us are to some extent neurotic, that "to be human," as Ernest Becker has expressed it, "is to be neurotic in some ways and in some degrees." It has, however, been pointed out that the artist, though by his nature more aware than others of the world's formidable presence, by virtue of his creative talent neutralizes the neuroses which such awareness brings. The psychology of satiric art has yet to be fully explored. The common assumption that a work of satire is a direct expression of the satirist's state of mind is usually bound up with the further assumption that his state of mind during the creative act was one of profound disgust; the satirist, it is generally believed, has been giving unmediated expression to his own emotional disturbances. And yet, with some of T. S. Eliot's remarks in mind, could we not hold with just as much probability that the satirist is finding release from these disturbances? His creative talent, that is, has made it possible for him to distance his distressing emotions by placing them within the patterns provided by the distinctive structures and language afforded by traditional satire. Furthermore, the aggressiveness that lies at the heart of satire, the assertion of contempt, the expressed determination to destroy a threatening enemy bespeak in some degree public attitudes held in common by the non-enemy. The satirist's voice, Swift's voice, is frequently as much a communal as a private one.

Needless to say, there is no way of determining the extent to which Swift, as a practicing satirist, can be said to have discharged his personal and impersonal anxieties. But if he gained a measure of relief, there are tensions of a kind from which, as one profoundly aware of existential realities, no complete escape is possible. What is above all characteristic of Swift is his refusal to accept the pleasing illusions that screen from us the truth about ourselves, our myths, and our institutions. In *A Tale of a Tub* we are told of a sect that believed the universe to be a large suit of clothes and man himself a microcoat or "complete suit of clothes with all its trimmings." If we are to believe the psychoanalyst Otto Rank, the normal man and the spiritually neurotic one differ in that the former can "successfully ... repress, displace, deny, rationalize, dramatize himself and deceive others," whereas the latter has arrived at that point to which psychoanalysis would bring him, namely, "the point of seeing through the deceptions of the world of sense, the falsity of reality."[31] Psychologically the spiritually neurotic is nearer the actual truth than is the person of so-called normal experience. It is the truth from which he suffers, like the satirist who has composed *A Tale of a Tub*, constantly probing beneath appearances.

Conspicuous among the anxieties that are part of the civilized person's experience are those attributable to a given historical situation. In his *Thoughts on Religion* Swift declared (1) that a man must believe according to his reason, (2) that no man is bound, save by his reason, to believe, (3) that one is not accountable to God for the doubts that arise in his own heart, since these are the consequence of the reason he has implanted, and (4) that want of belief "is a defect that ought to be concealed when it cannot be overcome." The *Thoughts* have often been taken to be a confession of his own lack of faith, a defect which he felt compelled to hide beneath silence and outward conformity. But these and similar observations of his are open to a different construction, and according to this one they are essentially impersonal, the tensions of belief which they register being such as were widely felt in England during the seventeenth century—more particularly during the post-Restoration decades—by those whose faith was, as they termed it, a rational one that lay between the unquestioning and unquestionable dogmas of the Roman Catholic tradition and the sheer inspiration of the extreme nonconforming sects. It was John Locke's desire to establish more firmly the grounds of this rational faith that originally sent him on his explorations into the workings of the human understanding. That at the close of his life he felt compelled to acknowledge the weakness of human reason and had come to place sole reliance on the words of Christ as given in the Gospels is striking illustration of religious anxiety induced by certain historical circumstances. Swift, like Locke, rejected both Roman Catholic faith and the enthusiastic visions of the sects.

He accepted the Anglican rational faith. Yet for him, too, reason fell short of our needs; religious doubts still arose; and in all the affairs of life it was tragically apparent that man himself was not a rational being, only one capable of reason. While Locke, in consequence of his theory of human experience and development, rejected the concept of original sin, Swift was bound to a certain Calvinistic pessimism, as another passage in his *Thoughts on Religion* tells us: "Miserable mortals: can we contribute to the *honour and Glory of God?* I could wish that expression were struck out of our Prayer-books."

4　Swift the Writer
Some Approaches

A number of somewhat different approaches to Swift the writer lie open to us. There is always the biographical approach, and in the course of the brief sketch of Swift's life given in the second section of the present essay many of his important works have already been cited. But there are other ways of treating his writing, and these sometimes allow important aspects to come more prominently into view.

His career as a writer can, for instance, be read with reference to successive situations of an intellectual-psychological character in which he found himself. The earliest of such situations is to be associated with his first years at Moor Park (1691-93) and the half-dozen formal verse pieces he managed to produce before he took leave of his Muse in utter discouragement. His poetry of this time has little to recommend it in the way of effective, let alone graceful, statement, but is nevertheless important because of what it has to tell us about Swift's early views and convictions. He was still inexperienced as a writer, and he had yet to catch sight of the possibilities that an ironic style of delivery opened up, but already he saw himself as one destined to be a satirist, and had furthermore defined in his own mind the chief distempers of the time calling for correction.

The *Ode to Sancroft* (1692) is particularly revealing. As Archbishop of Canterbury, Sancroft had refused to take the oath of allegiance to William and Mary, out of loyalty to the Church, and early in 1690 had in consequence been deprived of his office. In eulogizing Sancroft for standing firm in his principles—though no supporter of James II, Sancroft felt nevertheless that in the Church's eyes William and Mary could not be lawful sovereigns—Swift voiced a kind of absolute moral-religious idealism that he was reluctant in later life to express openly. Truth, he wrote, is eternal, the first of God's attributes, above the "giddy circumstance / Of time or place"; our world is but the "dusky shade" of Heaven. The Church must not be led blindfold by the State; it is above the State, showing "the way which leads to Christ."

A different ambiance marks the final years at Moor Park. The Swift who returned to the Temple establishment in 1696 was no longer a frustrated poet. He had suddenly found himself. Prose, not verse, was now his medium; wit, impertinence, dazzling irony replaced the humorless earnestness that had characterized the early poetry. It was with a superb self-assurance that he set to work on *A Tale of a Tub*. In his early verse he had shown himself to be a satirist of sorts. In the *Tale* he greatly extended his scope, introducing a serio-comic psychology of folly and madness, and above all employing new satiric techniques and schemes to produce the most extraordinary effects. Ideas and principles, brought to life as people, engage in mock contests; and there is irony everywhere, turning sense to nonsense and back again to sense. Throughout the three compositions that make up the book that was to appear in 1704—the *Tale* proper, *The Battle of the Books*, and *The Mechanical Operation of the Spirit*—Swift is engaged in his own remarkable way in defining what he has come to see as the norms of civilization in religion, in literary culture, and in science and philosophy, and *per contra* in making open war against adverse forces posing a threat to humane culture. The elaborate machinery of the satire, differently designed in each of the pieces, serves to drive his judgments home with humorous, sometimes brutal, force.

Never again does Swift exhibit quite the same exuberance of spirit, the same play of wild satiric imagination.

For Swift, the years between his return to Ireland in 1699 and his decision in 1710 to give his support to the Tory ministry presented a new and distinctive situation. The English political scene in the aftermath of the events of 1689 was one of excitement and uncertainty against a background of repeated electoral contests. The Whigs and the Tories were battling each other for power; the Dissenters were demanding an end to all discrimination against nonconformity; the Established Church was not of one mind concerning its position and proper authority in the post-Revolution political society. Swift, often in London, was able to keep abreast of national affairs. Soon he was commenting in print, anonymously in every case, on the pressing issues of the day. In 1701, in response to the attempt by a Tory House of Commons to impeach several prominent Whig statesmen, he came forward with a pamphlet entitled *A Discourse of the Contests and Dissensions in Athens and Rome,* in which he cautioned the Tories against yielding to violent partisanship, and proceeded to outline his own political concept—owing something to Locke and a good deal to Temple—of a balanced constitution in which the interests represented by the Lords on the one hand and the Commons on the other were held in balance by the Crown.

Modern assessments of the *Discourse* differ sharply. Yeats admired it greatly. It was, he wrote, essential for the understanding of Swift: "It shows that the defence of liberty boasted upon his tombstone did not come from political disappointment . . . and what he meant by liberty."[32] Frank H. Ellis, on the other hand, in his scholarly and definitive edition (1967) of the *Discourse,* materially reduces Swift's ideological originality and the depth of his convictions by viewing the pamphlet as one of the many that appeared in 1701, one issuing from a background of tangled intentions and interests on the part of both the writer and the political groups involved. Moreover, in describing the style of the *Discourse* as political rhetoric used for the immediate purpose of discrediting the Tories, Ellis further diminishes the intellectual significance of Swift's performance. Altogether, the *Discourse* has suffered such a decline in reputation that one writer questions whether it deserves the modern scholarly edition that Ellis has provided.

But when the broad context within which the *Discourse* rightly belongs is kept in mind, Yeats's evaluation of the pamphlet is borne out. The 1699-1710 period marked Swift's appearance as a writer on matters of public interest. His motives were no doubt mixed. Unquestionably he hoped to rise in the world by bringing himself to the notice of people of influence. Also, he was by this time a practiced writer flexing his muscles, eager to prove that his command of style extended to the kind of rhetoric which effective discussion of public issues demanded. But most of all, as Yeats splendidly recognized, he had things to say, convictions to define that had immediate bearing on contemporary questions. In the *Discourse* he was affirming, against both Hobbes's absolutism and High Tory doctrine, the Whig theory of government, which declared the people as a whole to be the ultimate source of power in the state, and it was this concept of liberty— freedom by tradition, freedom under established law—that he carried into his own later Toryism.

Among his many other pamphlets of this period, all of which can in one sense be seen as exercises in skillfully pointed rhetoric, his *Sentiments of a Church-of-England Man* (its appearance was delayed until 1711) deserves a place alongside the *Discourse* as a timely paper concerned with yet another issue before the public, viz., the proper relationship between the post-Revolution State and a still-Established Church. Swift was here adopting a tone of moderation though insisting that there were religious elements embodied in the Church which were by their nature beyond reach of the State.

The writings of these years, taken together, should remind us that there is a Swift who has often been lost sight of—a man who in no way impresses us as psychologically disordered but rather as a person concerned with the outside world rather than himself and who saw his role as that of an informed commentator offering his views on some of the urgent problems facing his contemporaries.

The nature of Swift's political writing underwent a dramatic change when, in the autumn of 1710, he allied himself with the new Tory ministry of Harley and St. John and became its chief publicist, soon entrusted with the editorship of the all-important Tory journal, the weekly *Examiner.* If Swift's motives in cutting his ties with the Whigs included any that were self-centered, these were outweighed by two entirely impersonal considerations: he had come to believe that it was to the Tories that the Church would have to look for support; and he was one of a growing number who were persuaded that the war with France—the War of the Spanish Succession, underway since 1702—had been unduly prolonged and must be brought to a speedy close. The Tories were now dead set against the war and were prepared to negotiate a peace. In his many short publications, in his papers appearing in *The Examiner,* and in *The Conduct of the Allies,* a lengthy and carefully planned pamphlet timed to appear just as Parliament, in December 1711, was preparing to vote on the question of peace, Swift drew without scruple on all his remarkable resources as a rhetorician to drive home the Tory antiwar policy, to place responsibility for the war upon the Whigs, and to represent the present opponents of peace—in particular the Duke of Marlborough, the Allies' great general—as wishing to prolong hostilities for their own personal, material gain. The ruthlessness with which Swift employed all the stratagem of *ad hominen* rhetoric as he sought to crush the opposition by the sheer force of his pen inevitably raises some question as to his intellectual honesty. Was Swift genuinely persuaded of the truth of what as a polemicist he was proclaiming with such a show of passionate conviction? The answer is that he assuredly was. To him war in all its aspects was never anything but abhorrent, while in Marlborough and those around him who were determined to block the way to an immediate peace he saw a group reaching for excessive power and ready to destroy the balance of interests in the nation, a balance on the maintenance of which justice and freedom depended. We have to recognize, on the other hand, that no political writer as completely committed to his cause as Swift can remain unaffected by the blind animosities to which he is constantly exposed. Too often and too readily, we feel, Swift yielded himself up to unreasonable rancour and prejudice, though rightly enough his reputation as a consummate political controversialist survives.

Swift was forty-six when he returned to Ireland in 1714 shortly after Queen Anne's death and the fall of the Tory ministry. Some twenty-six years of activity still lay ahead of him before the infirmities of old age finally overcame him. Instead of languishing in Ireland as another might have done, he succeeded in mastering the seemingly unpropitious situation in which circumstances had now placed him. He found new interests and cultivated old ones. His resourcefulness as a writer remained as great as ever. He turned to verse with renewed spirit. He wrote essays both on general topics and on more purely literary matters. Most if not all of *Gulliver's Travels* dates from the earlier 1720s. Furthermore, he found it impossible to remain aloof from public affairs, and in Ireland's discomforts, for which the selfish and shortsighted colonial policy of the English government was chiefly responsible, he found a new cause to take up. In pamphlet after pamphlet he drew attention to the plight of the Irish and the injustices imposed on them by England, while also upbraiding the Irish themselves for their incredible lack of initiative regarding such remedial means as lay open to them. The *Drapier's Letters* (1724) and *A Modest Proposal* (1729) are, with reason, the best remembered of the Irish writings. Swift's immediate purpose in the *Drapier's Letters* was to prevent Wood's halfpence from circulating in Ireland and to force the authorities in London to withdraw the patent of authorization, and in this he was triumphantly successful. Dean, Drapier, and Patriot, he had become a national hero. As effective public rhetoric, the *Drapier's Letters* is to be seen as perhaps his most impressive achievement; each letter is pointed with infallible aim at a particular audience, and fashioned in style, language, and way of reasoning to insure the maximum effect. But Swift's mind was set upon more than immediate victory over Wood and his copper coins: in the famous fourth *Letter—To the Whole People of Ireland*—he spoke for political freedom everywhere, then and thereafter. Likewise in the case of the *Modest Proposal,* though the immediate situation being addressed was that of Ireland's economic ills and the widespread suffering they caused, the protest which the ironic means of delivery raises to a level of terrifying intensity is far wider in its impact, extending to man's indifference to social-economic injustices whatever the circumstances.

In following Swift through the period dating from 1714 we can observe a change of presence on his part. It is always difficult to know precisely what image of himself, or what images, Swift entertained in private. What we so often see is a public image he chose to project. He had a natural instinct for self-dramatization, and this became more apparent in his later years, his public image more distinct. The values here are subtle. He recognized in himself the national figure that he had now become. There was pride in his achievement as a writer, perhaps a greater pride in what he had championed and what he had succeeded in accomplishing as an active participant in the political and social actions of his time. But the view he presented of himself was a multi-angled one. The pride was hedged with irony, opportunity being accorded to others—sometimes his friends, sometimes his detractors—to voice their own judgments of him.

What for want of a better term can be called the Swift theme runs strongly through the poetry written after 1714. Swift, we are told in *The Author upon Himself* (1714), "had the Sin of Wit [,] no venial Crime." What he understood "wit" to be, what "humor" and "raillery"—three terms current at the time which he applied to his own work—we learn from *To Mr. Delany* (1718): by wit

is onely meant
Applying what we first Invent:

> What Humor is, not all the Tribe
> Of Logick-mongers can describe;
> Here, onely Nature acts her Part,
> Unhelpt by Practice, Books, or Art.
> For Wit and Humor differ quite,
> That gives Surprise, and this Delight:
> Humor is odd, grotesque, and wild,
> Onely by Affectation spoild,
> 'Tis never by Invention got,
> Men have it when they know it not.

Raillery, here attributed to Voiture, is defined as irony "which turns to Praise."

In *A Dialogue between an eminent Lawyer and Dr. Swift* (1730), Swift is being urged by his friend the lawyer to fall in with prevailing opinion and celebrate for "learning, probity and truth" certain well-regarded writers whom Swift abominated. Swift responds to such advice with a kind of indignation:

> Must I commend against my conscience
> Such stupid blasphemy and nonsense?
> To such a subject tune my lyre
> And sing like one of MILTON's choir,
> where DEVILS to vale retreat
> and call the laws of wisdom fate,
> Lament upon their hapless fall
> That force free virtue shou'd enthrall?

But the poem, instead of ending with these lines echoing in our ears, closes with the lawyer's ironic observation: some, misled by philosophers, must honour you alive and dead, some must acknowledge your irony and wit; some must dread your pen; some must hate your person:

> And you on DRAPIER's *Hill* must lye,
> And there without a mitre dye.

Of all the poems associated with the Swift theme, the one that has always attracted most attention is his *Verses on the Death of Dr. Swift* (1731). It is a masterpiece of commentary—self-commentary in one sense, but self-commentary effected as often as not through the things said of him on the occasion of his imagined last illness and death, by friends, acquaintances, and people knowing him only by reputation. Some are indifferent to his passing, while others speak of him in detraction; the one whose long and detailed character sketch of the Dean extends through the final third of the poem is eloquent in defense and praise. The *Verses* has recently been the subject of much critical discussion, directed chiefly at the closing section, with its eulogistic portrait of Swift. The praise, it has been objected, is being bestowed in an exaggerated manner, and statements are made that are in flat contradiction of what lies in preceding sections of the poem.[33] Was Swift at fault, betrayed into giving free rein to an eager defender? Before we let ourselves be persuaded that he was, we ought to bear in mind the description of the defender as "one quite indifferent in the Cause," and of his character sketch as an "impartial" one. It is hard to believe that the Swift who, we are told, was the first to refine irony and to show its use is not showing its use in this vehemently partial eulogy, where the intended effect of the irony is one of wry humor. But if such irony as this is present here, it comes and goes, and much that is being said is not being undercut by it:

> "The *Irish* Senate, if you nam'd,
> "With what Impertinence he declaim'd!
> "Fair LIBERTY was all his Cry;
> "For her he stood prepar'd to die;
> "For her he boldly stood alone;
> "For her he oft expos'd his own.

How, on the other hand, are we supposed to take such lines as the following?

> "He knew an hundred pleasant Stories,
> "With all the Turns of *Whigs* and *Tories:*
> "Was chearful to his dying Day,
> "[If] Friends would let him have his Way.

It scarcely needs to be said that the biographical approach to Swift the writer and the slightly different one just taken are not the only possible ones. The others tend, however, to be somewhat more narrowly focused. Swift's scattered and his more extended observations on style, the characteristics of his own prose style, and the position he may be said to occupy in the history of English stylistic theory and practice during the latter part of the seventeenth century and the earlier part of the eighteenth are perhaps too specialized subjects to be of general interest, though their importance becomes increasingly clear in the light of modern research in the linguistic and stylistic fields, and several interesting stylistic studies of Swift have recently been made.

There is, however, one topic which, though in a strict sense one of the narrower ones, is central in everyone's recognition of Swift the writer. We know him chiefly as a satirist—one of the greatest of all time. The nature of his satiric art is a subject of foremost importance, and is best approached in terms of his characteristic stratagems and techniques. The ensuing section takes up such matters.

5   Swift's Satire through Irony

From the first, Swift saw himself as a satirist. In his early verse—the Moor Park compositions of 1692 and 1693—we find him flailing away at modern follies, at "learned Vanity," and the "Censure, Pedantry, and Pride" threatening at that time to overwhelm the guardians of true learning; he decries the state to which Philosophy has been reduced by the fools and madmen into whose hands she has fallen; he turns upon all those who in following false guides miss the true way, "the way which leads to Christ," calling them "Mistaken Idiots"; he describes his hate as a lash which "just heaven" has decreed "Shall on a day make sin and folly bleed." His themes were ones which had been occupying the attention of satirists and critical commentators since the time of the Renaissance and Reformation—themes pertaining to intellectual and religious values, old and new. A clear line extends from Swift's early verse into *A Tale of a Tub,* the latter concerned, as Swift pointed out, with "the numerous and gross Corruptions in Religion and Learning."

Yet despite certain thematic similarities, the poems and the *Tale* might just as well be the work of two different authors. Between the time he left off writing verse and the time he turned to his first prose satire Swift had somehow managed to acquire another posture and a new language. He was no less the satirist, no less bent on the chastisement of modern idiots and madmen at large in the precincts of learning and religion, but he had learned the use of wit, humor, imaginative ingenuity, and of irony above all. The sin of wit—"Swift had the Sin of Wit no venial Crime," he wrote in a later poem— informs the *Tale* from start to finish.

If Swift's readers, past and present, have sometimes been left bewildered by the apparent complexities of the *Tale* and other satires that followed, if they have disagreed among themselves as to the right interpretation of, for instance, the final book of *Gulliver's Travels,* the reason for this lies mostly in their failure to grasp Swift's highly individualistic manner of satiric expression, consisting essentially of certain recurring stratagems and rhetorical forms. Direct satire such as we find in the early verse is straightforward moral condemnation; it may be forceful, but it proceeds wholly without humor or wit. True, Swift never entirely abandoned this direct mode, and some of the most powerful of his later poems are scathing attacks, all wit forsaken, on individuals and groups that had earned his hatred. But in the greater prose satires he committed himself to another kind of satiric statement, witty, indirect, and unfolding in accord with certain of his favorite formal devices.

Before we turn to those devices that he most frequently employed and consider the ways in which he customarily manipulated them, we should do well to reassure ourselves that his impelling purposes are never in actual fact obscured by the satiric stratagems he resorted to, no matter how lacking these may be in straightforwardness. The complications he introduced may prove distracting in places and now and then throughout a whole piece, but the satires, when followed with reasonable care, do not leave us in the dark as to his genuine intentions. Only the most obtuse reader could fail to recognize that *A Tale of a Tub* is a multitargeted satire, unmistakably aimed at modern "corruptions" in religion and learning: at modern writers, modern critics, the irrational spirit finding expression in certain religious zealotries, modern scientists when guided by exclusively materialistic assumptions, etc. *A Modest Proposal* is proclaiming as clearly as any of Swift's entirely nonironic pamphlets the deplorable conditions to which Ireland had been reduced by English blindness and English greed combined with the lethargy of the Irish themselves; it even lists, by way of patently ironic dismissal, a number of measures that might readily be taken to promote the general welfare. Nor is *Gulliver's Travels* in much different case. Our responses to the ingratitude of the Lilliputians and their other unlovely qualities that eventually disclose themselves is in no way uncertain. Gulliver's recital of what he believes to be and would have the king of Brobdingnag believe to be the enviable features of European civilization has left no one doubtful as to the intended meaning. The follies encountered during the third voyage are never anything but priceless and unambiguous examples of the absurdities to which men will commit themselves when they take leave of their senses. The controversies which have arisen among present-day critics over the right interpretation of the fourth book of the *Travels*[34] might seem to call in question the assertion that Swift's overall purposes are never, in fact, obscure. The problems of interpretation raised by Gulliver's account of his sojourn in the land of the rational horses are special ones, and more will be said about them further on in the present section, but until then one appeals to what ordinary readers having little familiarity with today's sophisticated criticism generally find in the *Voyage to the Houyhnhnms*. To them the satiric message is surely not, as some modern critics would have it, that reason as cultivated by the Houyhnhnms is here the central absurdity. A writer in *The Dublin Magazine*, Daniel R. Brown, has remarked that Swift has sometimes been made more complicated than he must have thought he was; a person wonders "if he can trust his own reading ability when there are so many contradictory explanations of Swift's intentions."[35] If the Houyhnhnms are sometimes gravely comical creatures, they operate nonetheless as symbols of the kind of reason—essentially an ethical reason—which underlies all of Swift's moral concepts and constitutes his satiric norm.

The key to those of Swift's satires that proceed by indirection lies in his use of irony. He made no secret of the fact that he looked upon himself as an ironic writer, but regrettably he failed to point out exactly wherein his irony lay, thus leaving it up to us to find out. Irony, which essentially turns on the gap between appearance and reality, has taken many different forms of expression. There is an ironic manner of speaking, in which we say one thing but mean something else. Irony in drama entails the sudden recognition of an actual state of affairs on the part of one or more of the characters who up to the moment of enlightenment have not known the truth. The classical rhetorician distinguished as one of the set devices at the command of the writer and the orator the ironic figure of speech, productive of something allied to sarcasm. In a Renaissance work such as Erasmus's *Praise of Folly* the irony is chiefly one of situation, human wisdom and wise folly, but the sense of irony as a figure of rhetoric, a publicly defined verbal scheme, lingers on. It is this rhetorical aspect that we must not lose sight of in taking stock of Swift's irony.

To cast ridicule upon his mistaken idiots and rascals Swift would often take up a position inside their psyches, entering into their irrational notions and misguided desires and allowing their beliefs and their beloved practices to unfold themselves in all their perverse fullness and baroque complexities. This kind of ironic acquiescence in folly is of frequent occurrence in the satires, and more often than not it takes that special form of irony which shapes his most memorable satires. In these Swift's imaginary characters—each, in the language of recent Swift criticism, a persona of distinctive character—are in charge, sometimes throughout an entire satire, sometimes more briefly. Time and again it is they who are addressing us, they who have written what lies before us; what comes to us is their biased statements. Much of *A Tale of a Tub* consists of the words and thoughts of the modern writer who dominates section after section of the satire. The supposed writer of the *Modest Proposal* presents himself as a well-intentioned citizen motivated solely by a concern for the common good. Lemuel Gulliver is the narrator throughout the account of his four travels to strange lands. These characters have been endowed with qualities that render them irogenic: the modern exhibits an enthusiasm for anything and everything that is new, and in consequence becomes the zealous advocate of much that is ridiculous in recent endeavours in letters and learning; the public-spirited author of the *Modest Proposal* is able to view society and its problems solely in the light of the new statistical science, which cannot distinguish between human beings and cattle and which deals with both in exclusively quantitative terms; Gulliver on many occasions exhibits a naiveté that leads to erroneous conclusions about people and things confronting him. Furthermore, the various ironic misapprehensions on the part of these characters are being driven home by means of two rhetorical patterns referred to in Swift's time as "praise by blame" and "blame by praise," its mirror image.[36] Swift's satire as delivered indirectly through one of his personae proceeds ironically not only in the sense that the presiding figure lives in a world where things as they are have been turned upside down but in the further sense that what he singles out for praise is seen to be blameworthy and what he blames actually calls for praise.

It should be recognized, however, that Swift's irony raises a good many important questions which the foregoing discussion leaves unanswered. Why, for one thing, was he so strongly drawn to irony? Was he responding to something deep within him? Was irony implicit in his view of human nature and the human experience? From everything we know of him it is evident he saw men as creatures forever allowing themselves to be misled by mere appearances, willfully turning away from reason. Both fool and knave were to be exposed as the living ironies they were. It was not a case, as today's absurdists would have it, of rational human beings condemned to live in an irrational universe. The universe was rational; the irrationality lay with human beings.

Another kind of question is this: as a satirist, what did he gain by irony that he could not have achieved through condemnation untouched by anything ironic? A good deal—such is the indisputable answer. Irony invited imaginative wit—witty imagery, witty analogies, witty distortions of the obvious, amusing and sometimes lethal parodies; it introduced complications and moments of temporary bewilderment for the readers, all of which created a peculiar excitement and tension; it was a way of amplifying and dramatizing the underlying satiric message. The simple and literal meaning of *A Modest Proposal* could be conveyed in a few direct and impersonal statements; delivered in ironic code as an extended argument for putting children to a novel and laudably practical use, it has become a masterpiece of satiric statement.

A problem constantly arising concerns Swift the ironist in relation to his reader. Did he intend his irony to be followed without too great difficulty, or was he challenging his readers to find their way through the mazes he had constructed? Since we can have no direct knowledge of what in these respects was going on in his mind, we have to rely entirely on the works themselves. To reaffirm a point already made, there is no satire of Swift's in the ironic manner—with the possible exception of *A Voyage to the Houyhnhnms*, to be discussed in this connection later on—that can be said to leave a reasonably alert reader in the dark as to its informing purposes. Unquestionably there are passages that perhaps seem needlessly—or ought one to say purposefully?—confusing, but with some effort these can usually be untangled, and sometimes there are surprises awaiting us. Swift liked to pull the rug out from under us, and we should not be caught off guard by a certain trick of his which results in a doubling of the irony: in an instant the voice changes; unannounced, there is a shift in the point of view; the persona who has been holding forth is suddenly transformed into the satirist himself, and it is he who is now speaking to us and is speaking without irony—what up to the moment when the shift occurs has been the subject of praise on the part of the persona and thus has been indirectly exposed as blameworthy is now being declared reprehensible in a direct and unequivocal manner. This trick is sometimes executed in reverse fashion, false blame suddenly turning into genuine commendation. With a still further turn of the screw, Swift on occasion allowed his persona to hold up to ridicule what is in truth ridiculous—or to praise what is indeed admirable—but to do so on entirely mistaken grounds.[37] The irony is simultaneously cutting both ways, as in *The Mechanical Operation of the Spirit*—which follows *The Battle of the Books* as the third satire given in *A Tale of a Tub*—where a scorn that matches Swift's own is being directed against religious enthusiasm, but by a supposed writer who, like some of this writer's friends among the modern virtuosi, is a complete materialist to whom everything about religion is ridiculous.

The way one approaches the whole subject of Swift's irony depends in some important respects on the view one has of him as a writer writing. The present discussion up to this point has asked by implication that he be taken as a satiric artist who stood at a certain distance from his creation—a writer, that is, who went about this business in an impersonal way, intent on achieving his desired effect through calculated craftsmanship. Among contemporary Swift critics there are those, however, who reject such an approach as cold and unimaginatively academic. For them the essential Swift is to be understood only in what others would describe as romantic terms, with great significance being given to his emotional life, and stress being laid upon the assumed emotional origins of his writings and their self-expressive aspects. It has recently been suggested that there is to be found in Swift a bitterness which he turned not only against himself but also, in the manner of Baudelaire, against his readers, he and they alike implicated in the ironic condition, all in some degree sharing an inescapable guilt.[38]

Such an interpretation of Swift as a writer and of his satire and irony lies open, however, to a serious objection: namely, that the concept of literary art which was part of Swift's entire intellectual and literary inheritance did not invite self-involvement of the author nor encourage an expressionistic kind of writing. To whatever degree Swift as a person may have sensed his own moral and spiritual weaknesses, as a satirist he was not giving vent to his own guilt feelings. He was holding up to ridicule and condemnation the sins and follies of the world, and in doing so he was fulfilling what had long been understood to be the function of the satirist. This assault on knavery and folly was, furthermore, assumed to be in the nature of a public act publicly endorsed, the satirist's readers shared in the contempt and anger being directed outwards. It is difficult for us today to understand the determinant factors in an artistic tradition such as this, so different from what now prevails, and many reject what is spoken of as literary neoclassicism, because of its supposed coldness and life-denying formalisms. Yet in Swift we have one who manifestly eludes the charge of aloofness, and for that reason we are tempted to attribute to him characteristics that are romantic rather than neoclassical. What we fail to understand is that he was in fact a neoclassical artist by virtue of a controlled and objective manner of expression which nevertheless had behind it the deepest convictions and succeeded in communicating a sense of the perpetual crises, internal and external, confronting civilized men.

It is easy to understand why more has been written about *Gulliver's Travels* than about any of Swift's other works. As a commentary on the human scene it ranges over a great number of topics of perennial interest, and it does so in most provocative ways. It remains forever fascinating, open to widely differing interpretations.

It can be said, however, that today there is general agreement among Swift's readers and critical commentators that irony is at work in many parts of *Gulliver's Travels*, sometimes in quite obvious ways, though surprisingly there have in the past been many who, judging by their recorded observations, remained completely unaware of the presence of anything at all ironic. In the first place, we have come to recognize in Lemuel Gulliver one of Swift's personae. He is not the kind of substantial character given us by writers who are observing the traditional formulae of fiction; he is not a free being, seemingly self-activating, but instead a figure that quite patently is being manipulated by his creator: he is one sort of observer in Lilliput, another in Brobdingnag, and a still different one in the country of the Houyhnhnms. Each of his four travel accounts has its own slant. Gulliver's reactions are ironically relative to the different situations he finds himself in.

And there are more obtrusive ironies. For example, in the *Voyage to Lilliput* the little people, as Gulliver in the end discovers, are not what at first they seem to be, quaint and harmlessly ridiculous, but equal in malevolence to people of normal size. In the *Voyage to Brobdingnag*, Gulliver's peevish assessment of Brobdingnagian civilization is a clear case of ironic praise by blame, the blame being accounted for by the mortification inflicted on Gulliver by the King, who has just pronounced Gulliver's fellows in England and Europe generally to be a "most pernicious race of little odious vermin." The episode in Part III concerning Gulliver and the immortal Struldbrugs is one of ironic misconception followed by bitter enlightment.

But what of Part IV? There was a time, now past, when everything in the *Voyage to the Houyhnhnms* was taken in an almost literal sense: Gulliver was assumed to be Swift, Gulliver's sentiments were those of Swift the man, Gulliver's detestation of the Yahoos and the reverence in which he held the Houyhnhnms signified Swift's own unconscionable hatred of the human race for its failure to live up to an impossible ideal. In Thackeray's words, Swift was "filthy in word, filthy in thought, furious, raging, obscene." We no longer labor under this kind of perverse misapprehension of what it was that was guiding Swift in perhaps his single most powerful satiric stroke. This does not mean, however, that Swiftians have today reached agreement on the fundamental meaning of the fourth Voyage. Far from it. For the past half century a battle of the critics has been under way in the learned periodicals devoted to literary studies. The matter principally at issue concerns the Houyhnhnms and the

Yahoos and what they are supposed to be symbolizing. There are those on the one hand who hold fast to the more traditional interpretation according to which the Houyhnhnms represent, beyond peradventure, the life of reason, the Yahoos the rejection of all that distinguishes men from beasts. Taking issue with these traditionalists are those critics who have been vigorously disputing the traditional Houyhnhnm equation.[39]

In the view of those committed to the later, revisionist interpretation, Gulliver is not only a persona—most critics regardless of which side of the debate they support now agree on this point—but one who here in Part IV is being used ironically and to an end which in the past has not been rightly perceived; Gulliver's ideal horses—such is Swift's message— are not ideal creatures, and their vaunted life according to reason is in fact a lifeless, closed existence; the celebration of the Houyhnhnms is diminution if not downright dismissal by mistaken praise. In short, it is the Houyhnhnms that are the real objects of Swift's satire. It has sometimes been maintained, too, that Swift's purpose in all of this was to direct us to a middle way of existence lying between an all-constrictive reason and utter irrationality, and it has been suggested that Pedro de Mendez, the kindly captain of the Portuguese ship in which Gulliver is finally conveyed back to England, has been brought into the story as a reminder that such a mean is not beyond the reach of everyday human beings. The most striking conclusion arrived at by certain of the revisionist critics has to do with the famous finale of the last Voyage. Older readers, more often than not, regarded the ending as the most terrible of all Swift's satiric visions; T. S. Eliot, for instance, described it as "one of the greatest triumphs that the human soul has ever achieved,"[40] moving us to pity and a kind of purgation, and compelling us to feel everywhere "the tragedy of Swift himself."[41] But some who follow the more recent line of commentary see the climactic episode of the *Travels* as comedy. In his obsessive desire to be a horse can Gulliver, they ask, be taken as anything but a figure of sheer absurdity?

The ongoing discussion of Part IV has taken a slightly

different course as a result of what R. S. Crane[42] and, more recently, C. T. Probyn[43] have brought to light concerning the historical background of some of the factors present in the *Voyage of the Houyhnhnms*. For Crane and Probyn the immediate point of departure is that portion of Swift's letter to Pope of 29 September 1725 that bears on *Gulliver's Travels*. "I have ever," Swift wrote,

> hated all Nations professions and Communityes and all my love is towards individuals for instance I hate the tribe of Lawyers, but I love Councellor such a one, Judge such a one for so with Physicians (I will not Speak of my own Trade) Soldiers, English, Scotch, French; and the rest but principally I hate and detest that animal called man, although I hartily love John, Peter, Thomas and so forth. this is the system upon which I have governed my self many years (but do not tell) and so I shall go on till I have done with them I have got Materials Towards a Treatis proving the falsity of that Definition *animal rationale;* and to show it should be only *rationis capax.* Upon this great foundation of Misanthropy (though not Timons manner) The whole building of my Travells is erected: And I never will have peace of mind till all honest men are of my Opinion . . .

It was Crane who called attention to the fact that the definition of man which Swift sought to disprove was the definition found in the standard seventeenth-century textbooks on logic: *Homo est animal rationale*. Further, the textbook that Swift was undoubtedly familiar with, as Crane was able to show, was the *Institutio Logicae* by Narcissus Marsh, provost of Trinity College, Dublin, during Swift's early undergraduate days there.

C. T. Probyn, taking up where Crane left off, has explored two further aspects of the intellectual background of the Voyage. (1) The distinction Swift made in his letter between man as a species and individual men is to be found as far back as Aristotle. (I may add the following to Probyn's discussion. A certain John Sergeant, a confirmed Aristotelian of Swift's time, insisted that only individuals are "Entia" or "things," and that Man, or Rational Animal, should be "divided intrin-

sically" between those who have more and those who have less
of the faculty of reasoning.)[44] And it is this crucial distinction
that Gulliver fails to grasp. He has no sense of the individual,
and oblivious to the good qualities of a Pedro de Mendez, con-
ceives an all-embracing loathing of Man. (2) The Houyhnhnm-Gulliver-Yahoo triad of names and concepts devised by
Swift is a variant on the Man-Horse-Monkey triad of terms used
by Aristotle, and in Swift's day by English writers on logic, to illustrate, apropos of syllogistic reasoning, the distinctions between genus, species, and individual. What Swift did was to
create in the fourth Voyage an imaginative fantasy in which these
distinctions operate in an ironic way. "The result," as Probyn
very cleverly puts it, "is a grotesque and vexing syllogism, in
which Gulliver is the undistributable middle term." Is he, in
other words, of the Houyhnhnm kind, the members of which
are uniformly and magnificently rational? Is he Yahoo, a species
bereft of reason and uniformly loathsome?

In the discussion of Part IV—discussion that has been en-
livening so much of modern Swift criticism—the ironic factor
has not, needless to say, been overlooked; the wholly literal
interpretation of *Gulliver's Travels* is now a thing of the past.
Yet the degree to which irony has structured the entire Voyage has not always been perceived, and frequently the fundamental ironic meaning has been misinterpreted. There is a
steady driving force operating everywhere in the *Voyages,* and
only when this is clearly discerned does the full meaning of
Gulliver's experiences among Houyhnhnms and Yahoos
emerge. As we have already seen, satiric irony is present in
the first three parts, where it comes and goes, taking various
forms according to the occasional situations arising along the
way. In the final *Voyage* it does not come and go; it informs
the entire piece. Here Swift was drawing upon all of his past
experience as a satiric ironist to fashion an absolutely unique
statement concerning the human moral situation. Gulliver is a
persona; he is trapped in an agonizingly ambiguous situation
between the Houyhnhnms and the Yahoos, turning from the
latter in utter loathing, seeing the former as beings of unri-
valled excellence. He errs in assuming that *all* Houyhnhnms
are admirable, and again in jumping to the conclusion that

only Houyhnhnms have been endowed with excellent qualities. Yet we who are following Gulliver's account are not to
dismiss or mistake everything that he reports concerning the
beliefs and practices of the Houyhnhnms. They do indeed
embody—or would if wholly imaginary figures ever could—
much that is admirable. Surely their great maxim "to cultivate
reason, and to be wholly governed by it" is in itself in no way
ridiculous. Blame accrues to Gulliver because of his undis-
criminating praise of the Houyhnhnms, yet paradoxically his
praise is by no means all blame. Gulliver is a fool by reason of
his inability to distinguish between individual and species.
Hence, for him, European man is detestable Yahoo. Hence
his ultimate lunacy; he cannot be a Houyhnhnm, but he
consoles himself by conversing with his two stone-horses at
least four hours every day.

Be it observed, finally, that the irony that embraces Lemuel
Gulliver reaches out beyond the fourth book of the *Travels*.
Houyhnhnm or Yahoo? Our human pride is checked as the
question haunting the hapless Gulliver comes home to us who
are readers. But it is brought home to us as only irony is able
to do, the end effect of which is neither that of tragedy nor of
comedy but of something that suggests both yet is distinct
from both. In Pascal's *Pensées*, with which Swift was in all
probability familiar, one comes across a statement which in
substance can be said to anticipate the one being made by
Swift, save that Pascal's proceeds quite without irony:

> It is dangerous to show man too clearly how much he
> resembles the beasts without showing him his greatness.
> Likewise it is dangerous to let him see his greatness
> without his lowness. It is more dangerous still to leave
> him in ignorance of both. But it is greatly to his advan-
> tage to show him both. Man must not think of himself as
> equal either to the beasts or the angels, but he must not
> remain in ignorance of the two aspects of his nature; he
> must be aware of both of them.[45]

Reading this, we become aware of what it is that Swift has
accomplished through his ironic mode.

Pascal's words are also a reminder that Gulliver's surrender
to despair is Swift's call to action and his declaration of human

freedom. Man, neither beast nor angel, is yet capable of
rational acts. He is free to strive with all his might for whatever promises to promote the human estate.

6   Swift the Augustan
Order and Freedom

Swift's significance as an Augustan figure extends well beyond his achievement as a satirist. He entered tire-
lessly, sometimes passionately, into the affairs of his time, as
his public life in England and later on in Ireland attests. In
numerous pamphlets, essays, sermons, occasional observations and thoughts, he addressed himself to the pressing
issues and problems then facing the nation. There were questions of a political nature, questions concerning religious beliefs and practices, questions as to the relationship of Church
and State, on all of which Swift held firm views. The writings
in which he set forth these views and defined the convictions
and principles which they carried with them constitute a truly
remarkable record. Here for Swiftians and intellectual historians alike is the ideology of a distinguished Augustan. Swift,
as we know, had a hearty contempt for intellectual systems
and system-makers, and he had no intention, we may be sure,
of constructing a system of his own. Much of the time he was
drawing upon the concepts embodied in what is broadly referred to as the Western tradition of Reason and Nature; he
was an Aristotelian of sorts; he knew the Renaissance
humanists; he found much to admire in Bacon; he was
strongly influenced by those seventeenth-century English
writers dedicated to the ideal of reason in religion and of
freedom in political society, and who sought to restrain the
religious enthusiasts in their midst and at the same time to
refute Thomas Hobbes, whose theories seemed a denial of all
their liberal and human values; he was closely familiar with
Sir William Temple's political thought. For his part, Swift
succeeded in putting forward in an uncommonly coherent

and consistent manner the assortment of ideas which had taken root in his mind and were pertinent to the times. He was, to be sure, only one Augustan, first a Whig and afterwards a Tory, an Anglican priest dedicated to the defence of his religion and his Church, a spokesman for social order and political liberty, and a satirist in pursuit of the everlasting fools and knaves of this world. His vision was limited in ways which by our time are easily recognized, and to many people his general world-view has seemed, as it did to George Orwell, a ridiculous one. But the values and principles constituting what for him was a clearly defined central position all reflected, whether we find ourselves in sympathy with them or not, the Augustan experience as it was realized in one of the great personalities of the period.

Swift's thinking on most of the matters of foremost concern to him seems to have been firmly shaped by the time he left Moor Park in 1699, and in two compositions of the early years of the new century, the *Contests and Dissensions in Athens and Rome* (1701) and *Sentiments of a Church-of-England Man* (written in 1708; published 1711), he set forth with great clarity a range of ideas respecting government, religion, and the Established Church. In these publications he showed himself to be wholeheartedly in accord with the political principles embodied in the Revolution settlement, though as an ardent Anglican he viewed with something less than total approval the religious situation which had come to pass. He was still a Whig, not yet having gone over to the Tories, but in spite of his eventual shift of allegiance, his early political principles remained substantially unchanged through the years, while his religious position, as far as one can tell, was fixed unalterably by the time he took orders in the Church.

Of the two sections of the *Sentiments,* the first is given over to a discussion of religion and the nature and position of the Church of England, the second to matters of government, the point of view throughout both being that of a Churchman who accepts the post-Restoration order of things. The Church of England, we are told in the opening section, asks for belief in God, Providence, revealed Religion, and the divinity of Christ. Its government by bishops seems the fittest form, whether or not it is of divine origin—Swift himself believed that it was, as he indicated elsewhere. Its rites and ceremonies are not fixed unalterably, but there are no compelling reasons for changing them. Toleration of the sects— the reference is to the Toleration Act of 1689—is acceptable: the sects already exist throughout the nation, and furthermore the use of violent methods to enforce conformity would not be agreeable so long as these sects do not manifestly endanger either the government or the Established Church. Nevertheless, religious schism is always deplorable, and at the least constitutes a temporal danger in that those who are discontented in religious matters are ready, in the name of what they call true religion, to use their acquired power to destroy existing government in order to establish an order of their own in its place. It is absurd to argue, as some do, that God is delighted with variety in faith and worship. Some of those who argue for liberty of conscience do so in order to advance their own irreligious notions and thereby to "undermine the Foundations of all Piety and Virtue"; to allow such as these an unlimited liberty of the press is a positive scandal to government.

These convictions of Swift regarding the Church, and particularly his position vis-à-vis the nonconformists, are scarcely calculated to advance him in modern eyes. One thinks of Locke's generosity of spirit towards those of divergent views, and regrets Swift's uncharitable attitude. Yet we should not make the error of attributing Swift's steadfast opposition to the nonconformists to blind, unreasoning prejudice. His mind remained fixed upon the disorders of the Civil War and on what the Puritans had done to their opponents, and he saw at the root of all this the desire on the part of a ruthless minority to gain and wield unrestricted power. The result had been tyranny—as imposed by a single group upon the entire nation. The normal person, he had written in *A Tale of a Tub*, is content to pass his life in the common forms "without any thought of subduing multitudes to his own power, his reason, or his visions"; the one who would break with the established order, who would stamp upon his own party his particular notions, is one whose overheated imagination has assumed control over his reason. For Swift, order in society was primarily a psychological matter; it was that ascendancy of reason and common sense which corresponded to what in the experience of the individual was control of the irrational impulses and desires emanating from the lower faculties.

The latter section of the *Sentiments,* devoted to questions of government, contains by contrast nothing that one is likely to take exception to today. The principles that are being articulated here are in no significant respects different from Locke's. A Church of England man, wrote Swift, does not hold that any one of the different forms of regular government is more acceptable to God than the others, but it does not follow that all are equally suitable—every nation has its own character, every country its own climate, and these are perhaps determining factors. What is important above everything else is that the laws preserving persons' security be none but such as can be repealed by the whole people. The administration—that is, the executive power—may lie in the hands of one person or of several, so long as the legislative power, "which in all Government must be absolute and unlimited," remains in the entire people.

Political convictions of this nature were, as Swift was at pains to point out, in direct opposition to that theory of arbitrary power which Hobbes, along with those supporting the doctrines of the divine right of Kings, had once advanced. Arbitrary power seemed to Swift a greater evil than anarchy itself, "as much a *Savage* is in a happier State of Life, than a *Slave* at the Oar." "A *Slave* at the Oar." He was to use similar words again. Swift's concept of social order may have been a more constrictive one than we are willing at this day to view with any great degree of sympathetic understanding. Was not his kind of order the equivalent, in reality, of a hopelessly closed universe? It may at times seem so. But with the idea of order went his correlative idea of freedom, freedom to assert through words and action the inalienable rights possessed by civilized men in an ordered society. History tells us that order and freedom have never been fully reconciled, and the realism forced on us by twentieth-century world events suggests that they are never likely to be. But the effort to bring them into mutual accord has been and continues to be a part of our human adventure.

There is much in Swift's thought that will elude us unless we take into account as one of its potent elements that Anglican rationalism that had found many seventeenth-century exponents and was still present, though sometimes in an attenuated form, in the Augustan consciousness. Swift came to his rationalism not by way of any optimism regarding human nature and the human estate but through a kind of despair and horror. Man was a fallen creature. "Miserable mortals! can we contribute to the honour and Glory of God? I could wish that expression were struck out of our Prayer-books."[46] The words were those of Swift the priest, voicing his ingrained Christian pessimism. But the Anglicans influencing Swift had frequently sought to translate man's transgressions into behavioral terms, and to this end had employed the psychological principles and terminology that were then generally accepted. The human psyche in its normal, undisturbed state recognized order and followed the dictates of the reason implanted by God. Irrational behavior was the consequence of psychological disturbances: reason, which was the capacity to arrive at accurate distinctions and judgments, was overwhelmed by false visions and unregulated desires engendered in the unreasoning faculty of the imagination. Rationalism of this kind, which ends up by being mostly a theory of irrationality, is present everywhere in Swift. For him, religious nonconformity and political tyranny were both, as we have seen, manifestations of unreason, and it can be said that *A Tale of a Tub* exists through its preposterous enactments of irrationality in learning and religion.

The kind of reason which in the context of behavioral theory became a psychological faculty meant to exercise ethical control was by no means an exclusively Anglican concept,

and was common to European thought, though Anglican
writers, especially during the post-Restoration era, made
much of it in their treatises and sermons, and such writings
strongly influenced Swift. But it was reason of a somewhat
different order, lying in another context, that was the particular mark of seventeenth-century Anglicanism: its religious
beliefs were asserted to be reasoned convictions; reason
meant the logical operations of the intellect.

In some of his sermons and in various entries in the
Thoughts on Religion Swift expounded his rational religion in
clearly understandable language, but there is little here that
leaves much of an impression today. The religious issues that
were then real—they were so to Swift, beyond all doubt—no
longer present themselves as they once did. It was, rather,
Swift the satirist who injected life into the doctrines of the
middle way, notably in *A Tale of a Tub* with its allegory, comic
and malicious, involving brothers Peter and Jack, and
whenever he was moved thereafter to reduce enthusiasts in
and out of religion to figures of surrealistic folly. In the
rationalism that lay behind so much of his satire, reason in the
psychological sense and the reason of the middle way came
naturally together.

Of the several strands discernible in Swift's thought, one
that is constantly in evidence is the conservatism that colored
his outlook on the mores and fashions, social and intellectual,
of his time. What was new was in all likelihood merely some
manifestation of enthusiasm, unsettling the order that reason
and long practical experience had brought to pass. Swift
found the new science, much of it, undeserving of serious
attention. The modern developments in philosophy for which
Descartes and Locke were responsible falsified the way
knowledge is acquired and thus the very nature of knowledge. The new ethics then coming into prominence, which
took issue with the older view of human nature by asserting
man's innate benevolence, was, if not openly derided, rejected
by implication, and totally so by one who found the doctrine
of original sin confirmed in human history and who as a

satirist recorded the endless progress of sin and folly through
the land. To the new optimism which was gathering, as Englishmen appraised with growing satisfaction the benefits,
materialistic and otherwise, accruing in their post-Revolution
society, his response was anything but a receptive one.

Swift's position regarding science calls for a few comments.
No one is likely to enter a serious defense of his antiscientific
attitude, which stands in such sharp contrast to the position of
one like John Locke, to whom science meant more than anything else the exploration of the still-unknown properties of
our universe. Swift belonged to the school of humanists dating back to the Renaissance—humanists who believed that
man's rightful concerns lay not with natural phenomena but
with his own moral being, and who looked upon all scientific
efforts as so many examples of misdirected intellectual
energy. There had been much of this kind of anti-science on
the part of writers known to Swift, Sir William Temple being
one of these.

It is to be observed, however, that in the case of some of
these writers, that which had frequently been put down as
anti-science pure and simple was in fact not that but rather
the indictment of what seemed to be false science—that is,
projects foolishly conceived and which by their nature could
not possibly result in anything answering our practical needs.
For example Samuel Butler, the author of *Hudibras*, to whom
Swift owed something, had levelled his satire at certain members of the then recently chartered Royal Society not because
they were conducting scientific experiments but because so
many of their experiments seemed preposterous. In *The Battle
of the Books* the spider is a repulsive figure meant to symbolize
the entire scientific spirit, but Swift was at the moment intent
on mounting an all-out attack on moderns of every sort.
Obviously he never understood the nature of genuine science, and quite as obviously he had no desire to do so, yet his
sallies were often directed less against science *tout court* than
against the follies undertaken in its name. It is this Butlerian
type of satire, which had settled into something of an established type after the founding of the Royal Society at the

beginning of Charles II's reign, that so enlivens the account (in the third book of *Gulliver's Travels*) of the experiments being conducted at the Grand Academy of Lagado by the virtuosi resident there. At heart Swift was something of a Baconian in his feeling that the aim of science should be the relief of man's estate. Though the intellectual curiosity of genuine scientists and their impelling desire to extend the frontiers of human knowledge lay entirely outside his experience, he did assert the rights of common sense against all forms of overreaching scientism, and at least in this respect his position remains a valid one today.

Swift's rationalism is constantly confronting us. We must, however, avoid the error of using the term *rationalism* in a simplistic way. Swift's rationalism is to be seen as including various concepts and intuitions that arose within different areas of his concern. In religion it is to be identified, as has already and repeatedly been pointed out, with what may be called Anglican rationalism. In politics and government it defined that reasonable order in society which conferred freedom from the twin evils of anarchy and tyranny, both reducible to human irrationality. In the arts and intellectual endeavor generally it dictated avoidance of singularity, of the farfetched, of everything patently useless, and of novelty for its own sake. It gave rise to a behavioral theory centering on what was thought of as normality of conduct—conduct in accord with that moral reasoning accessible to everyone; divergencies from the normal were taken to be the result of disturbance occurring in our psychological faculties.

Human irrationality in Swift's eyes took a multitude of forms. One of these was enthusiasm in religion, the unforgivable folly of the sects. Another was the lust for power. In his formative period, it is reasonable to suppose, Swift experienced a profound shock as Hobbes's theory of power forced itself upon his attention. One was compelled to concede to Hobbes that the desire for power was a fact of human history, a constant occurrence. But it was a fact which reduced human nature to the bestial level. The exercise of naked power meant triumphing over all others and bending them to one's own will and passions. In government and society it was un-checked power that fathered tyranny of the one, of the few, or as sometimes happened, of the many. Hobbes sought in absolute government—specifically, absolute monarchy—protection against anarchy. Swift granted that no form of social order was conceivable that did not derive from and did not exist by virtue of power; it was a question of where this power had come to lie. The order imposed by tyranny was a denial of the rights inherent in the whole body of society, a denial of the freedom to live in the way of reason. Swift the satirist and moralist was quick to condemn, quick to reject, and he rejected much. Yet to hold, as some have done, that such negativism on his part amounted to a denial of life and was thus an unconscious death wish is to take too little account of the course of his conscious thinking. To an Augustan rationalist such as Swift the full life did not mean what it has come to mean today. Essentially, it was the life that men, by virtue of their inborn capability of reason, were free to pursue if they chose. The things that Swift rejected were the things which, set deep in folly and knavery, stultified life.

NOTES AND REFERENCES
INDEX OF PROPER NAMES

NOTES AND
REFERENCES

Introduction

1. The term "Augustan Age" has sometimes been used to refer to the entire period from 1660 to 1799, sometimes to the eighteenth century proper, and sometimes, as here, to the years from 1689 down into the mid 1740s. See James W. Johnson, "The Meaning of 'Augustan'," *Journal of the History of Ideas,* 19 (1958), 507-22

2. The reader should perhaps be advised that what is here being suggested about the background of Locke's thought reflects in some important respects what are largely my own views. There are well-informed students of Locke who probably regard Descartes as an influence to be reckoned with; perhaps mistakenly I fail to discern an important influence here. In his *John Locke, A Biography* (1975), pp. 100-103, Maurice Cranston discusses with considered restraint the matter of Locke and Descartes.

3. On the entire subject of empiricism, see the instructive and well-considered article by Anthony M. Quinton in *The Encyclopaedia Britannica,* 15th ed. (1974), Micropaedia, VI, 766-70.

4. See Quinton's article on empiricism referred to above.

5. See Charles Webster, *The Great Instauration: Science, Medicine and Reform, 1626-1660* (1975). Webster's discussion of Bacon's influence during the pre-Restoration decades, upon which I have drawn, is of first importance; Webster has detailed why and how certain of the Puritans gave enthusiastic support to Baconianism.

6. There are some historians of science who do not find Bacon's influence on the development of English science to be significant. For such a view Charles Webster (*The Great Instauration,*

p. 493) refers us to two articles by A. R. Hall: "Science, Technology and Utopia in the Seventeenth Century," in *Science and Society 1600-1900*, ed. P. Mathias (1972), pp. 44-45; and "Merton Revisited, or Science and Society in the Seventeenth Century," *History of Science*, 2 (1963), 1-16. According to Hall, what was truly important was the tradition of Continental science established by such men as Galileo, Kepler, and Descartes.

7. See Margaret C. Jacob, *The Newtonians and the English Revolution, 1689-1720* (1976).

8. My use of the term here and elsewhere in the present study will, I hope, be clear from the contexts within which it occurs. The semantic problems surrounding the term are considerable, a fact pretty generally recognized today. See, for instance, Raymond Williams, *Keywords: A Vocabulary of Culture and Society* (1976), s.v. *liberal*. My primary meaning points to that political tradition, long gathering, which found voice and effective action in the Glorious Revolution of 1689. In respect of such liberalism Locke and Swift stood close to one another. In the further sense of general open-mindedness Locke's liberalism was scarcely shared by Swift. British liberalism, political and social, of the nineteenth century and the twentieth is a somewhat different matter, as is our American multivalent liberalism.

9. Concerning Swift's attitude towards both Descartes and Bacon, see my article "Two Paragraphs in *A Tale of a Tub*, Section IX," *Modern Philology*, 73 (1975), 15-32.

10. See Phillip Harth, *Swift and Anglican Rationalism* (1961).

11. In eighteenth-century Scotland, for instance, the Enlightenment took a decidedly rationalistic turn; see Anand Chitnis, *The Scottish Enlightenment* (1976). The Enlightenment in America, the subject of such recent studies as those by Henry F. May (*The Enlightenment in America* [1976]) and Henry Steele Commager (*The Empire of Reason: How Europe Imagined and America Realized the Enlightenment* [1977]), must in many respects be differentiated from what I speak of as the English Enlightenment. And as far as the latter is concerned, it was not all of a piece; as the eighteenth century proceeded, there were developments leaning towards definitely rationalistic thought, though this trend can, when reduced to too simple terms, be overemphasized (for a careful and informative statement see D. L. Le Mahieu, *The Mind of William Paley: A Philosopher and His Age* [1976]); and the rise of Methodism at this time is a clear indication of how remote from the experience of vast numbers of English people was

anything in the nature of rationalistic rationalism, as it was from the temper of such representative men of letters as Johnson, Goldsmith, Christopher Smart, and Cowper.

12. The general view of the English Enlightenment which I have long held and which I am here advancing accords in many respects with what has been expressed by Donald Greene in several articles. See the following: "Augustinianism and Empiricism: A Note on Eighteenth-Century Intellectual History," *Eighteenth-Century Studies,* 1 (1967), 33-68; "What indeed was Neo-Classism?" *Journal of British Studies,* 10 (1970), 69-79; "The Via Media in an Age of Revolution: Anglicanism in the 18th Century," in *The Varied Pattern,* ed. Peter Hughes and David Williams (1971), pp. 297-320.

John Locke

1. See Kenneth MacLean, *John Locke and English Literature of the Eighteenth Century* (1936); also Ernest L. Tuveson, *The Imagination as a Means of Grace: Locke and the Aesthetics of Romanticism* (1960).

2. See A. H. Cash, "The Lockean Psychology of *Tristram Shandy,*" *English Literary History,* 22 (1955), 125-35; also Helene Moglen, *The Philosophical Irony of Laurence Sterne* (1975).

3. In the Introduction to *Locke and Berkeley: A Collection of Critical Essays,* ed. C. B. Martin and D. M. Armstrong (1968), C. B. Martin writes thus: "The serious study of Locke is not in fashion. . . . [He] is inconsistent, obscure and repetitious. If it were not for the abundance of first-rate and still suggestive argument in his work, we could safely forget him as an object of serious study, and leave him to be the occasional sport of the young."

4. *John Locke: Essays on the Law of Nature,* ed. W. von Leyden (1954); and *John Locke: Two Tracts on Government,* ed. Philip Abrams (1967).

   The magnificent edition of Locke's *Correspondence,* edited by E. S. de Beer, of which Volumes I and II (both 1976) have now appeared—the entire edition is to consist of eight volumes—gives, along with the rest of the correspondence, those letters contained in the Lovelace Collection. Though de Beer is not the first to print the items in the Lovelace Collection, he is the first to give all of them and to accord each its proper position, by date, in the total correspondence.

5. Kenneth Dewhurst, *John Locke (1632-1704), Physician and Philosopher: A Medical Biography with an Edition of the Medical Notes in His Journals* (1963).

6. Roland Hall and Roger Woolhouse, "Forty Years of Work on John Locke (1929-1969)," *The Philosophical Quarterly*, 20 (1970), 258-68 and 394-96. In *A Bibliographical Introduction to the Study of John Locke* (1930), Hans Oskar Christopherson reviewed the period before 1930.

7. See, for instance, the review article by Alan Ryan, "The 'New' Locke," *The New York Review*, 20 Nov. 1969, pp. 36-40.

8. J. D. Mabbott, *John Locke* (1973).

9. John Rogers, in a review of J. L. Mackie's recent study, *Problems from Locke* (1976)—a review in the [*London*] *Times Literary Supplement* of 14 Jan. 1977, p. 38—remarks that Locke's reputation as a philosopher has for some years been on the rise, and he cites three reasons for this: (1) the fact that Locke was "often the first to raise and attempt to answer questions in a distinctively modern idiom"; (2) the declining sympathy for the antirealist position taken by Locke's successors Berkeley and Hume; (3) the growth in the study of intellectual history: "Locke's place, together with that of . . . Newton, in the vanguard of the Enlightenment has been long acknowledged; but Locke is also at the zenith of the revolution of the seventeenth century."

10. Rosalie L. Colie, "The Essayist in His *Essay*," in *John Locke: Problems and Perspectives*, ed. John W. Yolton (1969), pp. 234-61.

11. G. S. Rousseau, "Science and the Discovery of the Imagination in Enlightened England," *Eighteenth-Century Studies*, 3 (1969), 108-35.

12. Entry under 5 Nov. (Dewhurst, *John Locke*, p. 89).

13. Entry under 22 Jan. 1678 (Ibid., pp. 100-102).

14. In his *John Locke, A Biography* (1957), Maurice Cranston is clearly of the opinion that Locke was at least in touch with various people involved in the pre-Revolution movement directed against Charles II and James II (see, particularly, Chap. XIX of *John Locke, A Biography*). E. S. de Beer, on the other hand, holds that there is no indication that Locke "was ever in any inner ring," and little that shows any interest on his part "in current politics before the Revolution" (Introduction, *The Correspondence of John Locke*, I [1976], xxxvi). In his review of de Beer's edition of the *Correspondence (Times Literary Supplement*, 11 March 1977, p. 274), K. H. D. Haley acknowledges the scarcity of references in the *Correspondence* to the political struggles of the period, but

is not convinced that Locke was as indifferent to public events as de Beer suggests.

15. Many biographies of Locke, some long, some brief, are available, and in the present résumé of mine I have drawn in various ways on many of them. My principal indebtedness, however, is to Maurice Cranston's *John Locke, A Biography,* though I hasten to add that I have admitted into my account certain opinions and have proceeded to draw certain conclusions that are my own and for which other biographies are in no way to be held accountable.

16. *The Correspondence of John Locke,* ed. E. S. de Beer, I, 123.

17. See note 4 above.

18. From one of Whichcote's letters as quoted in the article on him in the *Dictionary of National Biography* (rpt. 1937-38), XXI, 2.

19. Quoted by Cranston, *John Locke,* p. 200.

20. As quoted in *An Essay Concerning Human Understanding,* Dover ed. (1959), I, 9 n2. Henceforth referred to as *ECHU,* all references being to this edition.

21. See Cranston, *John Locke,* p. 327.

22. Given by H. R. Fox Bourne in *The Life of John Locke* (1876), II, 377-91.

23. Locke's position is discussed by E. J. Hundert, "The Making of *Homo Faber:* John Locke between Ideology and History," *Journal of the History of Ideas,* 33 (1972), 3-22.

24. There are many studies of Locke's thought by professional philosophers. Of recent ones, J. D. Mabbott's *John Locke* (1973) will be found extremely helpful by the layman. A still more recent study—this of a more specialized nature—is J. L. Mackie's *Problems from Locke* (1976).

25. See Laslett's Introduction, particularly iv, 2 (pp. 79-91) in his edition of *Two Treatises of Government,* 2nd ed. (1967).

26. Entry under 5 Nov. (Dewhurst, *John Locke,* p. 89).

27. Entry under 22 Jan. 1678 (Ibid., pp. 100-102).

28. See Chap. II, "Of the State of Nature," in the second of the *Two Treatises Concerning Government.*

29. From the opening paragraph of Chap. IV, "Of Slavery."

30. Theodore Redpath, "John Locke and the Rhetoric of the Second Treatise," in *The English Mind,* ed. Hugh Sykes Davies and George Watson (1964), pp. 55-78.

31. J. D. Mabbott is most helpful in pointing out the shifting emphases to be noted in Locke's various discussion of central moral principles. See his *John Locke,* Chap. 12, "Moral Principles."

32. See note 19 above.
33. For a view of Locke's position relative to the intellectual currents of his time that is somewhat different from mine, see John Redwood, *Reason, Ridicule and Religion: The Age of Enlightenment in England,* 1660-1750 (1976), pp. 100-103.
34. *ECHU,* IV.i.2.
35. See *ECHU,* "The Epistle to the Reader."
36. *ECHU,* IV.x.7.
37. *ECHU,* I.iii.9.
38. Quoted by Cranston, *John Locke,* p. 466.
39. Rosalie L. Colie, "John Locke and the Publication of the Private," *Philological Quarterly,* 45 (1966), 24-45.
40. As quoted by Peter King, seventh Baron King, *The Life of John Locke* (1829), p. 335.
41. Edmund Gosse, *History of Eighteenth-Century Literature* (1889), p. 96.
42. Basil Willey, *The English Moralists* (1964), pp. 201-2.
43. For a discussion of this and other such schemes, see James Knowlson, *Universal Language Schemes in England and France, 1600-1800* (1975).
44. Stephen K. Land, *From Signs to Propositions: The Concept of Form in Eighteenth-Century Semantic Theory* (1974).
45. See Murray Cohen, "Sensible Words: Linguistic Theory in Late Seventeenth-Century England," in *Studies in Eighteenth-Century Culture,* vol. 5, ed. Ronald C. Rosbottom (1976), p. 229-52.
46. See Murray Cohen, *Sensible Words: Linguistic Practice in England, 1640-1785* (1977), a full-length study significantly enlarging on the earlier article referred to in note 45 above.
47. *ECHU,* II.xi.2.
48. Basil Willey, *The English Moralists,* p. 204.
49. In *The Imagination as a Means of Grace.*
50. *ECHU,* III.x.34.
51. See note 30 above.
52. *The English Moralists,* p. 202.
53. The three articles are "The Social Language of John Locke: A Study in the History of Ideas," *Journal of British Studies,* 4.2 (1965), 29-51; and the two already cited, "John Locke and the Publication of the Private" and "The Essayist in his *Essay.*"

Jonathan Swift

1. Referred to by Maurice Johnson, "T. S. Eliot on Satire, Swift, and Disgust," *Papers on Language and Literature,* 5.3 (1969), 310-15.
2. George Orwell, "Politics vs. Literature: An Examination of *Gulliver's Travels,*" in his *Shooting an Elephant and Other Essays* (1950).
3. Many references to Swift are indexed in *The Complete Prefaces of Bernard Shaw* (London: Paul Hamlyn, 1965). Austin Clarke: his essay on "The Poetry of Swift" is given in *Jonathan Swift, 1667-1967: A Dublin Tercentenary Tribute,* ed. Roger McHugh and Philip Edwards (1967), pp. 94-115; "A Sermon on Swift" appears in *A Sermon on Swift and Other Poems* (1968), pp. 9-12. Joyce: see Chap. 4, "Swift: A Paradigm of a God," in James S. Atherton, *The Book and the Work: A Study of Literary Allusions in James Joyce's "Finnegan's Wake"* (1959). Samuel Beckett: see Frederick W. Smith, "The Epistemology of Fictional Failure: Swift's *Tale of a Tub* and Beckett's *Watt,*" *Texas Studies in Literature and Language,* 15 (1974), 649-72.
4. From the Introduction to *The Words Upon the Window-Pane* (1931-32).
5. Torchiana, *W. B. Yeats,* p. 122.
6. *Explorations* (1962), p. 325.
7. See my article "Two Paragraphs in *A Tale of a Tub,* Section IX," *Modern Philology,* 73 (1975), 15-32.
8. Myrddin Jones, "*Further Thoughts on Religion:* Swift's Relationship to Filmer and Locke," *Review of English Studies,* New Series, 9 (1958), 284-86.
9. Rosalie L. Colie, "Gulliver, The Locke-Stillingfleet Controversy, and the Nature of Man," *History of Ideas News Letter,* 2 (1956), 58-62.
10. Irvin Ehrenpreis, "The Making of Gulliver's Last Voyage," *Review of English Literature,* 3.3 (1962), 18-38.
11. This subject is discussed in section 5 of the present essay.
12. In *Modern Language Quarterly,* 25 (1964), 5-21.
13. In *Criticism,* 2 (1960), 134-49.
14. Again, see my article "Two Paragraphs in *A Tale of a Tub.*"
15. See "The Tragic Generation," constituting Book IV of *The Trembling of the Veil* (1922; included in *Autobiographies: Reveries over Childhood and Youth and the Trembling of the Veil* [1926]).
16. See Philip Roberts, "Swift, Queen Anne, and *The Windsor Prophecy,*" *Philological Quarterly,* 49 (1970), 254-58.

17. For these details and for some bibliographical references, see my article "Swift" in *The Encyclopaedia Britannica,* 15th ed. (1974), Micropaedia, XVII, 856-59.

18. In *Review of English Literature,* 3.3 (1962), 39-68.

19. *The Letters of W. B. Yeats,* ed. Allan Wade (1954), pp. 818-19.

20. *Publications of the Modern Language Association,* 91, (1976), 33-43. An article by Athon Murtuza concerns the present subject: see his "Twentieth-Century Critical Responses to Swift's Scatalogical Verse: A Checklist," *Bulletin of Bibliography,* 30 (1973), 18-19.

21. In *Determination,* ed. F. R. Leavis, pp. 78-108.

22. Rawson's articles and books having reference to Swift in one way or another are the following: (1) "Gulliver and the Gentle Reader," in *Imagined Worlds,* ed. Maynard Mack and Ian Gregor (1968), pp. 51-90; (2) "Order and Cruelty: A Reading of Swift (with some Comments on Pope and Johnson)," *Essays in Criticism,* 20 (1970), 24-55; (3) " 'Tis only infinite below': Speculation on Swift, Wallace Stevens, R. D. Laing and Others," *Essays in Criticism,* 22 (1972), 161-81; (4) *Henry Fielding and the Augustan Ideal under Strain* (1972); (5) *Gulliver and the Gentle Reader: Studies in Swift and Our Time* (1973); (6) a "Biographical Introduction" to Swift, in *Focus: Swift,* pp. 9-16; (7) "The Character of Swift's Satire," in *Focus: Swift,* pp. 17-75.

23. "The Character of Swift's Satire."

24. Ibid.

25. Ibid.

26. *Henry Fielding and the Augustan Ideal under Strain,* p. 45.

27. Ibid., p. 203.

28. "Order and Cruelty: A Reading of Swift (with some Comments on Pope and Johnson)."

29. *Henry Fielding and the Augustan Ideal under Strain,* pp. 19-20.

30. "Order and Cruelty," p. 55.

31. Otto Rank, *Will Therapy and Truth and Reality* (1936). Quoted by Ernest Becker in *The Denial of Death* (1973) at the beginning of his ninth chapter.

32. In the Introduction to *The Words upon the Window Pane.*

33. See the provocative article by Barry Slepian, "The Ironic Intention of Swift's Verses on His Own Death," *Review of English Studies,* New Series, 14 (1963), 249-56. Another interpretation of the irony of this price—an interpretation to which I am indebted—is given by Peter J. Schakel, "The Politics of Opposition in 'Verses of the Death of Dr. Swift,' " *Modern Language Quarterly,* 35.3 (1974), 246-56.

34. See James L. Clifford, "Gulliver's Fourth Voyage: 'Hard' and 'Soft' Schools of Interpretation," in *Quick Springs of Sense,* ed. Larry S. Champion (1974), pp. 33-49.

35. "Swift and the Limitations of Satire," *The Dublin Magazine,* 9.4 (1972), 68.

36. The most helpful guide to the ironic devices recognized by the writers and critics of Swift's time is Norman Knox's outstanding work of scholarship, *The Word "Irony" and Its Context, 1500-1755* (1961). In his *A Rhetoric of Irony* (1974) Wayne C. Booth gives considerable attention to several of Swift's writings, including *Gulliver's Travels.*

37. In the article of mine referred to in note 7, I have called attention to the manipulations of ironic statement as found in one of the central passages of *A Tale of a Tub.*

38. C. J. Rawson, "Order and Cruelty."

39. See the summary by J. L. Clifford in his article referred to in note 34 above.

40. "*Ulysses,* Order, and Myth," *The Dial,* 75 (1923), 481. This and the citation in note 41 are given by Maurice Johnson in the article referred to in note 1 above.

41. "The Oxford Johnson," *The Dial,* 85 (1928), 68.

42. A latter version of the statement by R. S. Crane is to be found in his "The Houyhnhnms, the Yahoos, and the History of Ideas," in *Reason and the Imagination: Studies in the History of Ideas, 1600-1800,* ed. J. A. Mazzeo (1962), pp. 231-53.

43. "Swift and Linguistics: The Context behind Lagoda and around the Fourth Voyage," *Neophilogus,* 58 (1974), 425-39.

44. *The Method to Science* (London: 1696), under Book II, Lesson III, no. 11, note.

45. Nos. 153-54 in the edition of the *Pensées* by Philippe Sellier (1976); in the edition by Léon Brunschvig (1965) it is No. 418 (see Vol. II, p. 316); in the edition by Louis Lafuma (1951) it is No. 236 (see Vol. I, p. 81).

46. *Thoughts on Religion* (*Prose Works,* ed. Herbert Davis [1941-59], IX, 263).

INDEX OF
PROPER NAMES

(References to Locke and Swift are not indexed)

145

COMPOSED BY THE CREATIVE COMPOSITION COMPANY
ALBUQUERQUE, NEW MEXICO
MANUFACTURED BY THE NORTH CENTRAL PUBLISHING COMPANY
ST. PAUL, MINNESOTA
TEXT AND DISPLAY ARE SET IN BASKERVILLE

Library of Congress Cataloging in Publication Data
Quintana, Ricardo.
Two Augustans: John Locke, Jonathan Swift.
Includes bibliographical references.
1. Locke, John, 1632-1704. 2. Swift, Jonathan,
1667-1745. 3. England—Intellectual life—17th
century. 4. England—Intellectual life—18th century.
I. Title.
B1297.Q56   192   77-91059
ISBN 0-299-07420-X